BEHIND THE WATERFALL

Atheneum   NEW YORK   *1990*

BEHIND
THE
WATERFALL

Chinatsu Nakayama

TRANSLATED BY
GERALDINE HARCOURT

Originally published in *1980* under the title *Koyaku no jikan* by Bungei Shunju Ltd.

Library of Congress Cataloging-in-Publication Data
Nakayama, Chinatsu, *1948*–
    [Kyoaku no jikan. English]
    Behind the waterfall / Chinatsu Nakayama; [translation by Geraldine Harcourt].
        p.   cm.
    Translation of: Koyaku no jikan.
    ISBN *0-689-12099-0*
    I. Title.
PL*857*.A*4174*K*613*   *1990*
895.6'35—dc*20*   *89-18437*   CIP

Atheneum
Macmillan Publishing Company
866 Third Avenue, New York, NY *10022*
Collier Macmillan Canada, Inc.

Design by Janet Tingey

10   9   8   7   6   5   4   3   2   1

PRINTED IN THE UNITED STATES OF AMERICA

Contents

STAR
TIME

1

The child was walking unnaturally, avoiding the cracks in the pavement.

The distance between cracks didn't match the length of her stride. It was too difficult to step on every other square, but it was also a bit of a bore to step on all of them. Combining the two methods, she was determined at all costs not to step on the cracks.

Men and women hurried by, neatly dodging her. Hardly anyone paid the slightest attention to a child walking in a funny way. It was the time of day when school got out and the street ran by an elementary school gate. As she tugged to the left against the weight of a big bag full of books, the bag's shoulder strap pulled askew the geometric pattern of her sweater. To preoccupied people on the street a child going home from school, even with a peculiar walk, was mere background to the next turning or the changing traffic lights.

One or two of those who narrowly missed colliding with the child did receive a faint impression. From the way she paced along, intent on the pavement and oblivious to her surroundings, she appeared to be pursuing some precious but elusive flash of inspiration.

It was a strange sight, yet not strange enough to single her out from the swirl of other miscellaneous impressions. The casual observer might wonder in passing whether a child has thoughts of her own, but no more than that.

Certainly the exercise of keeping off the cracks was stimulating a corner of the child's mind. It didn't produce anything so clearly defined as thought; more a kind of peristaltic movement, like that of the intestines.

It was too difficult to step on every other square, but it was also a bit of a bore to step on all of them. As she attempted to keep off the cracks that didn't match her natural stride, with every step the child's body recognized the lack of love in a world absolutely indifferent to her—a lack of love that she couldn't accept, nor adapt to, in any way. What she was actually doing now was probing the source of all those hurts that for some reason had steadily become part of her life, day by day, since the very first time her needs—for a hug, for a suck of the breast—had gone unmet.

The effort produced a queer sensation. Yet she didn't want to lose it. Once she had taken one step in this way, it seemed the next must not land on a crack either, nor the next after that.

Her steps rocked the sensation as if it were a containerful of water she was carrying before her. Bobbing to its surface only to sink again were new memories: incidents that had taken place at school that day. Several scenes bobbed up before her; nearly all centered on one small boy burned brown by the sun. All of her time at school was bracketed around what this boy was doing.

Arata had answered loudly while carving the corner of his desk; that was when the teacher had been calling the roll, running her forefinger down the black clipboard. Arata had reached over and said, "Lend me your eraser a minute"; that was when somebody was putting the answers to the sums up on the blackboard. And when Arata had carried in the big stew pan from the school kitchen, with only his eyes visible between the gauze mask and the clean white cloth covering his head, dishes were clattering all over the classroom.

Suddenly the child stopped. With a hint of agitation she turned her gaze from the sidewalk to the road and stared at the asphalt. There lay scattered fragments of thick glass from a car, each catching the sun like sticky crystals formed from the surface of the road. As she struggled to distinguish between the scene that had struck her and the agitation it caused, she was actually absorbed in the sight of the sparkling cluster. The crystals were so brilliant that her eyes lost focus and the light grew to fill them.

It had happened in the playground that afternoon. The green wire mesh between the school yard and the street cast a pale filter over the haberdasher's and the club opposite, the passing traffic, and the pedestrians occasionally turning to look into the school yard as they went. Only inside the encircling mesh did the incident take on its true shape and coloring.

During physical education, she'd been watching the boys' marathon while the girls waited their turn. Megumi from the clothing store had said to get their attention, "Let's see, who shall I root for?" At once Junko from the dry cleaner's had teased her: "Oh, everybody knows you're backing Sugimoto."

"Oh no, that's Michiko you're thinking of, isn't it?" Megumi had laughed, giving Michiko a dig with her elbow. With an answering grin, Michiko from the restaurant had slipped her arm through that of the child, who was standing next to her.

The girls had lost no time in getting cozily together as girls do, and the child had been moved to confide just loud enough for the others to hear, "I like Arata. Come on, Arata!" And then it had happened.

Megumi's plump, round face had looked back over her shoulder. The grown-up face of Michiko, who had linked arms with the child, turned toward her. Behind her peered the face of Junko, with her hair neatly combed.

Having turned to her all at once, her three classmates then turned away all at once and exchanged quick glances. The scene from that moment until Michiko let out a sigh was even more vivid now in the child's mind than it had been at the time. Her agitation was sharper, too.

An expression had been clearly visible on her classmates' faces, but the child could not understand it—to her it was a mask. A mask for which she didn't have a name.

Till that moment she'd been able to read their faces as easily as if they had been her own, and yet quite suddenly she couldn't understand. This was the first time that the child was aware that she'd been reading people's expressions; she also sensed where not being able to read them might lead, and grew desperate.

But before the child even had time to scan the three faces and try to work out their meaning, they had exchanged glances and come to an understanding among themselves. By the time Michiko let out that sigh, their expressions were no longer masks. The child knew only that the moment had passed.

Glancing at the boys on the running track, the three classmates had begun to compare their merits. Michiko's arm was still linked with the child's. It was as if nothing had happened. She even tried to tell herself that nothing had.

But now she simply couldn't keep hold of Michiko's arm in the same casual way. She had felt only too clearly a body heat completely separate from her own, a tepid warmth quite foreign to hers at the point where their skins touched. It felt as though the soft tepid mass, and the bone inside it, had accidentally gotten caught around her own arm. She had endured the unpleasant feeling, afraid to pull her arm away in case it might prove that something had happened.

What in the world had those masks meant? What in the world had they understood among themselves? And what sort of signal was that breath that Michiko had finally let out?

The child began to kick her left heel with her right toes as if to knock the answer out of it.

She kicked and kicked, but the answer didn't appear. All she understood was that somehow they had neither made fun of her nor condemned her. All she knew was that her own words and actions immediately before it had given rise to that momentary exchange, and that it had revealed something about herself.

The child thought over what she had said and done. She had called, "I like Arata. Come on, Arata!" She simply couldn't believe that that had been enough to set off the strange events of the next moment.

Every high-spirited young girl did the same. Given the slightest opportunity, they all declared which of the boys they liked. Then the others teased and carried on. The child had seen this happen several times a day. When she first arrived at this school, she'd been quite taken aback by these outspoken adult conversations that would never have taken place at her old school.

It had taken her a month or two to get over being surprised. She still didn't feel comfortable about this sort of thing, but if this was how it was done in Tokyo the child was willing to try and accept it. Though she hadn't wanted to transfer from her old school, now that she was here her instincts told her she should blend in quickly; that was why she had let the girls' confidences overcome the last of her hesitation this afternoon and had cheered on the boy. "I like Arata. Come on, Arata!"

Suddenly, something flared in the child's breast, sending its heat flashing through her body in an instant. The sense of something being wrong that she'd managed to overcome at the time surged back and shook her inside. As she stiffened against the wave of heat, the child realized that moment's meaning. It was simple. They had snubbed her by showing incomprehensible masks instead of teasing or carrying on in their usual way. The masks had whispered to one another, "How dare you be like us? You're different."

The wave of heat flooded her body with hopeless shame. She didn't think the snub had been at all unfair. There was no way she could hold a grudge against her classmates: they had welcomed her, the new girl who repeatedly came late and left early; they'd let her join in their games, and helped her and taught her the things she needed to know, and never once touched on the fact that this newcomer was a child actor. As long as she didn't do anything wrong, her classmates were always kind and gentle.

And today, clearly, she had done something wrong. What she did wrong was to be like them—she wasn't like them, she was different.

The child planted her feet firmly, clenched her fists, and stared hard at the shattered glass. She waited like this for the wave of heat and shame to subside. A passing car scrunched and scattered the fragments still farther with its firm rubber tires. Raising her head as if to follow the car with her eyes, the child began to walk with her normal stride.

The shame had subsided. The moment had sunk back beneath her other sensations, and in a vaguer, calmer state of mind she was remembering the tough kids at her old school.

Her first appearance on TV had been over two years ago, not long after Osaka got its first commercial station. It was merely the result of a chance acquaintance between a casting director who was looking for child actors and a friend of her parents.

Her performance, done almost as a joke, had caught the eye of the director and the producer and led to a second appearance. This led to another, and a year later the child was going from station to station, mixing with great old comedians and rising young stars.

The more public notice she attracted, the harder it became to stay inconspicuous at school, especially in view of the number of times she left early, arrived late, or took the day off. And at a time when it was still a luxury even to own a set, she was actually on TV.

Most of the teachers and parents disapproved of a child who appeared on TV, and their attitude made itself known to the other children. The only daughter of the owner of a small ironworks found it particularly hard to stomach, and with the confidence that came of being big and well built and excelling at sports, she organized the other girls so that one day they deliberately turned the child away from their lunchtime game of dodge ball.

True to their rules of etiquette, the child had called out, "Let me in!" and tried to join the players, but her way was blocked by the iron manufacturer's only daughter, who told her flatly, "No, we won't."

Looking down with hooded eyes at the bewildered child, she said as she turned away, "You think you're so smart because you're on TV. We're not playing with you anymore," then returned to the watching group of girls and called, "Okay, let's go," as she leaped into action. The girls followed her lead at once, some avoiding the child's eyes uncomfortably. She stood there dumbfounded. Nearly all the girls in her class were on the square dodge ball court. But not one came over to her. The lines of the court, traced with the toe of someone's sneaker, had become the magic circle she'd once read about in a book: it surrounded the girls and she could not break in. After a while she murmured under her breath, "So that's it." When she could find no other words to follow this, the child slowly turned on her heel and strolled over to the deserted area behind the school building where for a short time she cried her heart out. After she stopped crying, she remained there alone, leaning against the wall and idly running her tongue around the back of her teeth until the bell summoned her to class.

The child didn't tell anyone the full story of what had happened, not even her parents. Though it was humiliating, she felt it was only natural after all that she should be left out. But she didn't see this as any reason to give up TV. She had already fallen under the spell of acting and in fact would have happily quit school instead, but her parents would never allow that. There was therefore no point in telling anyone what had happened, for it wouldn't change a thing. Her silence was made easier by the fact that she knew something—the thrill of performing—that the other children could not even begin to imagine, and the faint sense of superiority that this gave her.

Her life seemed to go on unchanged after this incident. Her classmates didn't always leave her out. Only the iron manufacturer's daughter took every opportunity to challenge her; the others behaved differently on different days and occasions. There were even some who felt sorry for her and were friendlier than before. The boys, who would soon be the age where they shunned the girls' company, watched out of the corners of their eyes and pretended not to notice.

The child seemed quite unchanged. Her uncomplicated manner when she joined a game, her liveliness in the classroom, the way she stood up to every challenge, all had been there before. The one difference was that she stopped inviting others to join her. If they invited her to play, she played, and if they invited her to walk home together, she walked with them side by side. But she never asked anyone herself. And she never, ever, spoke the password that the children used when they joined the group, "Let me in!"

The lines of the dodge ball court were seared into her memory and they held her back. No matter how friendly her classmates might seem, the child sensed the line drawn with the toe of a sneaker between them and herself. They were little imps who on some sudden impulse would surely flee behind that line again. She wasn't going to stand there dumbly left out again, shut out by the magic circle reappearing in its full force.

In this way both the school and her classmates receded until they were part of the outside world for the child. So when a famous playwright issued a warm invitation to her, she was more than happy to set out for Tokyo and felt none of her parents' misgivings. Changing schools seemed a very minor problem beside the attractions of a good role. Not that she wasn't a little anxious, but schools and classmates would always remain for her merely a part of the outside world, a world from which she could disengage herself at any time.

Yet now, as she made her way to the theater district, the child remembered her old classmates and their explicit rejection with a sudden fondness. Although that had made her cry, her new classmates and their graceful rejection had made her ashamed. By crying she'd been able to compensate for the misery and vexation, but about shame nothing could be done.

"Darn, darn, darn!" As the shame that had subsided earlier threatened to surge up again, she strode along muttering to herself. Her schoolbooks slapped rhythmically against her back. The waves quickly receded behind her, taking with them many other scenes at school. Then the last of these sensations was swept away by the sounds of music coming from cinemas, familiar strains that told her the theater district would greet her around the next corner.

The short street contained a knot of two theaters, one music hall, and four cinemas, among which also lay a florist's, an ice-cream parlor, a restaurant, and a souvenir shop. Like passengers piled frantically into the lifeboat of a sinking ship, the buildings were all tumbled together, overlapping and bumping one another till it was difficult to tell where one ended and another began.

In every available space—between windows displaying fancy goods, glass cases holding wax models of the food on the menu, and windows revealing people inside drinking tea—were brightly colored signs of many sizes that hid the dirt and the patches on the old buildings.

Soon, once the cinemas had disgorged their matinée audiences, the theater doors had been opened wide, and the neon signs lit up the dusk to beckon the theatergoers in, the street would pulse with excitement, but just now only the supporting entertainers from the music hall stood outside its entrance. Having opened the show, they occasionally gave their barkers' cries as people passed briskly by.

Nearest to the corner were the entrance and the box office of a small theater. Over the box office counter hung a handwritten poster: *"By popular demand, now entering fifth record month!"* The billboards directly above and on both sides of the entrance (each of a different size and design) listed the child's name with the other actors.

When she turned the corner, the child slowed her steps as she always did and looked the signs over. On every one her own name occupied its same fixed position.

She was well aware that the actors' importance was indicated by their billings, the order of names set off here and there by dots or lines. She had also seen more than one fight over these positions on which the actors staked their futures.

There were seven actors billed above her on the signs. Below her there were four, plus the twenty-odd players lumped under the name of the theater company. For a mere child of eleven such a position was unheard-of. At the same time, if an adult actor had achieved as much popularity, that actor's name would already have been shifted two or three places higher.

Yet what swelled in the child's heart each time she saw the billboards registering her rank so rigorously was neither satisfaction nor resentment, but a confident anticipation of the day when her name would be moved all the way up to the very top billing. She hadn't exactly set her heart on it—she just felt a happy certainty that this was bound to happen some day.

While simply enjoying her roles and leaving everything to her talent and luck, the child hadn't failed to notice the misfortunes of those who remained in the lower ranks year after year, or the trials of those who made it to the top and then had a position to maintain; but she saw in these no relation to herself. In her own eyes the future promised by her name up there shone more gloriously than the name of the leading actress that presently occupied the top slot.

With a bounce the child broke into an energetic run. The fringe of her bobbed hair blew up and down over her round forehead. With the same energy she pushed open the heavy metal stage door, which was tucked away between the souvenir shop and a drink stand, and burst into the damp half-light within. Her shout of "Good morning!" echoed as she ran up the stairway beside the elevator. Behind her back the voice of the watchman returned this all-purpose greeting of those who begin work at night.

She climbed quickly, the soles of her feet pounding the concrete stairs that rose twisting and turning alongside a blank wall. The reverberations of her steps on the concrete traveled through the light that filtered in from the frosted glass of the landing windows. The child became so absorbed in the echoes of her footsteps that she didn't notice how dreadfully bleak the surrounding walls and ceiling and stairs were, nor that the back of the theater was terribly gloomy after its showy facade. She was overjoyed at letting her feet make all that noise—a noise forbidden during performances because it could be heard on stage.

She didn't pause until she reached the fourth floor. There she stopped her bouncing and on soundless feet entered a narrow corridor with oily floorboards. Like those on the floors below, the right-hand wall of this corridor was of varnished wood paneling. There were large sliding doors at intervals along it, and very soon the dressers would arrive just ahead of the occupants, slide the doors open, and hang in their place attractive strips of curtain dyed purple and red and primrose bearing the actors' names.

But with the doors shut tight the corridor wall was merely a stretch of shabby brown wood. While it remained empty, this fourth floor where the top actors had their dressing rooms was no different from the others. If she turned left at the far end and then walked straight ahead, she would come to the unlit wings of the stage, but the child stopped at the corner and peered into the cramped office partitioned off on the other side of the corridor: a bent back, clad in a dark-blue office uniform, and across the desk a forehead topped with close-cropped graying hair partly visible above a newspaper. Neither seemed to notice the child.

"Good morning."

The newspaper was lowered to reveal the features of a man nearing old age. The office worker turned, showing her middle-aged face powdery with high spots of rouge on the cheeks. She was evidently busy eating, for she nodded several times in the child's direction and covered her chewing with her hand. The elderly manager replied genially, "Ah, morning," glanced at the board where the cast's name tags hung, and added, "You're the first again today." Then he raised his newspaper once more.

The child had to stretch a little to flip her name tag over from the red to the black side. Hers became the only black name in the row of reds.

The clerk having swallowed her mouthful at last handed over a key from a large bunch. The simple key was so big it didn't fit into the child's hand. The wooden tag tied to the top was so worn that the corners were smoothly rounded and so engrained with dirt that the number could not be read.

The child turned back, gripping the key. She went along the oily-floored corridor past the shabby wooden walls and down the winding stairs beside the featureless walls, not making a great noise with her feet this time, but in a listless way taking the steps one by one.

The damp that rose from parts of the dreary old building and filled its air was creeping into the child's body.

It found its way in through her wide-open skin and made her feel old and damp.

On the second floor there was another oily corridor just like that on the fourth, the varnished paneling down the right-hand side containing one sliding door at the far end and two along its length.

The child fitted the big key into the rough keyhole of the middle door and turned it, then slid the door back with both hands, putting all her weight into it. The door was about twice her height, but after catching several times on its warped track it finally stood open.

The tatami floor mats of woven straw, which were the cheap kind without borders, were worn till they had a distinct nap and the matting surface was not much higher than the corridor floor. The wooden dividing walls on both sides were varnished like those outside, and several nails stuck out at various angles. The tarnished metal sash of the large window overlooking the main street looked impossible to open. A single square patch on the wall where something had been pinned for a long time still faintly retained its original whiteness, contrasting with the grubbiness of the fingerprints and tape marks around it.

In its age and dinginess the inside of this room was no different from the outside.

The child felt a certain amount of relief, however, once she got the heavy wooden door open. As if afraid that the air of the corridor would rush in, she hurriedly blocked it out with the door and hung the key from a nail in the wall.

Inside, at least, the air was everything a dressing room's air should be. Though it had lost some of its potency between the actors' departure the night before and the opening of the door just now, a suggestion of its lightness and gaiety still lingered.

The bulk and weight of the young actress who shared the room were still detectable in the brightly colored dressing gown hung from a nail in the wall and on the thick cushion covered in imitation crêpe placed before her little dressing table. The actress's shrill laughter and her visitors' small talk flowed in a soundless murmur from the bunch of overblown roses hanging over the mirror, the potted cyclamen, the colored ribbons saved from earlier bouquets and pinned in a row on the wall. The cloth draped over the dressing table (its lace border handmade by one of her fans) was permeated with the strong smells of powder and rouge and mascara and eau de cologne.

In the soft white light filtering through the frosted window and filling the room, all of these things seemed on the point of fading from sight as they awaited their return to life.

Placing her book bag beside her own dressing table—prettily done up by her mother in imitation of the actress's—the child slid face down onto the mats and there gave a groan and a stretch that seemed to wring out her whole body. A big yawn escaped her. As her fists slowly unclenched, she felt all the tensions pass out through her palms.

Her heartbeat thudded between the mats and her back. A thick reddish fog swirled inside her closed eyelids. Her lungs drew in careful gulps of the dusty-smelling air, and her skin savored the faint warmth.

The never-endingly repeated theme of *Plein Soleil* from the cinema opposite twined itself around her body, connecting with the same melody that had accumulated in every fold of her skin day after day, painlessly holding her still. Whirring pigeon wings skimmed above the faint noise of the streets.

The child felt her body buoyed up ever so slightly, then replaced firmly on the mats. Relief spread languidly through her.

This room, at this hour, seemed to be the only world in which she fit.

It was a crevice between things. It was the hollow of stillness formed by the boiling waterfall and the rock, it was the air pocket where two streams of turbulence meet. It was the point of contact between the lit-up streets and the dark, damp building; uproar cut off by a curtain of silence; night that had yet to drive out the day; a dressing room that had yet to become completely itself.

Here the child did not have to struggle. This place accepted her for what she was—the actress who wasn't a real schoolgirl, the child star who wasn't a real actress, the creature who was neither schoolgirl nor actress, child nor adult, but lodged in the crevices where those worlds met. It enclosed her like a skin and let her relax. It was the only place that did.

But the place was also uninhabited. There was no one here but herself. No matter what she felt or said or did here, there was no one to offer sympathy or opposition. This made her feel very lonely, and the child didn't like the room at this hour one bit.

Another yawn escaped, and she felt tears brimming in the corners of her eyes. She sat up abruptly, crawled over to her dressing table, and looked in the mirror.

Her eyes were not as full of tears as she'd thought. She tried feeling sad as she did in the play, which made the tears well up and almost spill over, but the moment she attempted to get a look at them overflowing the flood retreated again.

The round face in the mirror—a face far younger than she'd imagined—was inspecting her levelly with a disgruntled air. She raised and lowered her chin, turning her face to right and left until she found a particular angle and expression of the eyes, then she slowly removed her sweater while looking on in satisfaction.

Her sweater and shirt peeled off together and slipped over her head. Her reflection maintained the angle and expression of the eyes that she'd just found. This, she had decided, was her most adult, most beautiful angle and expression, but the childishness and scrawniness of the face went badly with the bare chest and its quite full breasts. The odd combination made the child miserable. She tried two or three variations of the angle of her face, but finally gave up. When she did so she looked more than ever like a confused child, making even odder the contrast with her breasts.

Though there was really no need to pretend she wasn't embarrassed, she averted her eyes and got up, muttering "Brrr! It's cold!" She put on the dressing gown she took from the wall, then plumped down at the dressing table again, this time turning her profile to the mirror. The low table covered in orange linoleum sat there, flat and blank, in front of her.

"I wish Mother would hurry up," she thought. The hour when her mother usually arrived wasn't far off, but this morning she'd said as the child had left for school, "I've got something to do first today, so I might not be there in time for curtain." This was no problem, since the child was accustomed to dressing herself and doing her own makeup. But she hated being alone until the actress who shared the room arrived.

Her father in Osaka came to mind, followed suddenly by the thought: how long will this play run, and then what will happen to me? It was the first time she'd asked herself these questions.

When her mother had brought her to Tokyo, she'd been full of excitement at having a good role, but nothing more. She'd had some vague notion that, like a roller coaster ride or a Disney cartoon, after a certain time it would turn into a happy memory that brightened the past, while new times would come along just like the old ones.

If the play had closed after a month as scheduled, it might have happened that way. The child might have boarded the Tsubame express and left the capital behind her, going home to the house where her father waited and to the school yard where the iron manufacturer's only daughter ruled.

But after more than four months, there was no sign of the play closing; it was a spectacular success and was set for a long run. A long run was also intended for the new TV series in which she would star on the strength of her success in the play, and there was a string of other TV shows and movies being planned.

Whenever the famous playwright set eyes on the child, he told her his hopes and gave her advice on her future career. The other adults treated her in the same way; only her mother, while too close to be sure of what was best, would try to see that the child wasn't cut off from her old life.

For the first time the child wondered, "What will happen to me after this?" To have discovered the pleasures of performing and to believe, as a result of the playwright's and everyone else's expectations, that one day her name would be given top billing in a blaze of glory: to look forward to these things meant the new times would not be just like the old ones, it meant choosing her own life. She had just begun, however indistinctly, to realize this.

"What will happen to me?" the child wondered, and stopped there. An unfamiliar heaviness weighed on her chest and prevented the doubt growing. The hard little bud of doubt sank into her inner darkness.

She was becoming lonely again. Pulling her book bag over, she got out her pencil case with a rough impatience that was secretly directed at her mother for being so late. She opened a textbook on the orange table and started on her arithmetic homework. Before long the tricky numbers and their crazy dance occupied her totally.

2

The shadows had been chased from the room by overlapping circles of fluorescent light. Darkness, tinged by neon colors, stuck tightly to the outside of the big window and tried to suck out the overheated, stuffy air.

As she skillfully applied cold cream to take off her street makeup, the actress was filling the air with cigarette smoke and her lovely voice.

A small woman in the head scarf and print apron with huge pockets worn by all the dressers made a cup of instant coffee for a man who was visiting the actress. This young director sat crosslegged, looking uncomfortable; between his sips of coffee the actress's darting glances were thrown back by the mirror and impaled him.

Meaningless items of small talk flew back and forth, taking on meaning. Like a baby sparrow, the child brightly pecked them up.

Forty minutes until curtain and the dressing room was now every inch a dressing room; the whole building had come back to life. From the room at the end of the corridor the old actor could be heard coughing and scolding his apprentice, while the voices of the walk-ons in the communal dressing room next door sounded through the wooden wall. The ceiling and the floor gave off other signs of the presence of many people working on the play as they climbed the yellow-lit stairs and squeaked along the corridors.

"You're turning into quite a beauty, aren't you?" the young director said with an amused look at the child applying her dark greasepaint and handling the sponge just as expertly as the actress. The child beamed and without pausing at her work said coolly, "Flattery will get you everywhere," a retort currently popular among the cast. If her mother had been there she certainly wouldn't have been allowed to get away with it. But the actress, the director, and the dresser laughed unconcernedly. Picking her timing, the child pressed her advantage: "You're just being nice to me so you can keep coming here whenever you like. Isn't that right?"

Delivered in an intentionally childish singsong, this line found its mark, provoking a loud laugh from the actress and a blush from the young man. He smiled wryly. "You've got me all figured out." Her laughter ending in a sigh, the actress let out a puff of smoke and said, "It's hard work ingratiating yourself with this kid. Who's your favorite, sweetie, out of the people who come to see me?"

Without a moment's hesitation the child gave a name. "He always brings cakes, and I get to have some."

"Say you like me, too."

"Well, you're not bad, I suppose, because you tell me stories."

In fact, she looked forward to the director's visits. They were fairly frequent, and he would often wait for the actress's return while she was on stage. With nothing to do, he would pass the time telling the child a funny story.

He always told the same one, about a man who kept a pet snake. The man loved this snake very much, but once he went away without it, and when he got home the snake was so happy to see its master again that the moment he opened the door it flung itself about his neck, and the man died. The child always laughed a lot, and begged to hear the story again next time. Although he was tired of it by now, the director had nothing else to talk about to an eleven-year-old. If he'd been more interested he might have thought up other funny stories, but instead he repeated this one whenever she requested it.

"The trouble is," continued the child, "it's always the same old story."

The actress laughed again at the director's startled look. The child's laugh was triumphant.

"So I'll have to try out some new techniques on you, huh?"

At this remark the dresser doubled over where she knelt, smothering her laughter against her decorously folded legs, and the actress smiled broadly as she smoothed her beautiful bare shin with the palm of her hand. The child picked up a mirror and hid her face, pretending not to have heard.

She had no precise knowledge of what he meant by "techniques," but she was alert to a subtle change in the adults' mood that gave off a danger signal.

As she lined her eyes in the mirror she was in good spirits. Her eyes reflected her satisfaction at having handled herself well, having gotten through the hardest part skillfully.

The child viewed most adults as a kind of mousetrap whose mechanism she didn't understand. She'd realized this after having it snap painfully shut a number of times on her careless fingers.

Her classmates had been one kind of trap, but a much simpler one. All she'd had to watch out for there was the dodge ball line. But try as she might, she couldn't locate its adult equivalent. Not having grasped even the helpful clue that children are egotists who think only of themselves, while adults are egotists who tend to think they're thinking of others, the child found adults to be completely random, completely baffling.

To adults, on the other hand, she herself was an unsettling creature. The deception that was stage acting didn't go with their idea of childish innocence. And a child who did it so well could hardly be anything other than sinister.

While they gasped in admiration at the child's stage presence, the way she got her lines down after a couple of readings and came through an all-night rehearsal more wide-awake than themselves, the adults couldn't help being revolted by her unchildlike behavior. In their eyes there was something unnerving in the contrast between the little girl who trailed around after them carrying her rag doll, and the cool professional onstage who would play a scene better than she'd been coached to do without any sign of nervousness.

Not knowing what to make of the child's split personality, the adults of the company behaved toward her just as other adults did, that is, according to the mood of the moment. There were times when they enjoyed her precocity and her mischievous practical jokes as if they were party games to enliven the tedium. At other times they might be annoyed by the pesky, noisy, cheeky brat. They were truly fond of her as long as she was obedient, and loathed her when she pushed herself forward. And as long as she stayed quiet, they tended to forget she existed.

Her mother tried somehow to impress on her that it was safer to be forgotten.

"Now, dear, don't go talking and joking to the grown-ups. If you're spoken to, just answer properly. That's all you need to do."

Every time some tale about the child's behavior came to her mother's ears, she would give her these instructions. As an adult herself, her mother could readily imagine how deep a trap envy would dig for a child on her way to fame and prestige in a world where adult and child worked as equals.

"Speech is silver, but silence is golden," her mother told her. But the child could not learn from the warnings.

Unless she approached people herself, they would forget her. And then, for a creature who is neither schoolgirl nor actress, child nor adult, there'd be only one place left to go.

That place was the uninhabited space filled with white light. A space where nothing moved except her reflection in the mirror. That very safe, very lonely place.

It was constantly at her back, creeping closer with soft fingers and trying to wrap itself around her. But the thought of being covered in that sensation like a snug second skin was worse than lonely—it was terrifying. The place might always exist, but she wasn't going to let it cover her over, all alone.

There were plenty of people in the outside world if she would just approach them herself. Though they might not be able to come into that place with her, they'd form a link with the outside world that meant she wouldn't be totally swallowed up.

As long as she had that link and could cling tight to the nearest part—any part—of the outside world, she could escape her fear of being swallowed by that place.

Thus the child had acquired the knack of approaching her classmates while keeping her eye on the dodge ball line. She had developed a sharp sixth sense, had polished her skill at running between the mousetraps whose mechanism she did not understand and helping herself to little bits of affection. When one snapped shut, she frantically jerked herself free and kept moving, seemingly unaware of the blood and pain and torn flesh.

She didn't see this as particularly hard. On days when it went well, like today, it was a sort of game. Not that she was actively enjoying it. She was simply too busy spinning something for which she needed the glances of other people and their hands reaching out to her—spinning something essential to her survival.

There was a hesitant tapping on the wooden wall. When the dresser answered, one corner of the pink curtain that bore the actress's name dyed in white lifted a little, and the old actor's apprentice showed his timid face.

"Sensei wants you to come for a moment."

The child answered brightly and, with a quick inspection of her finished makeup, scrambled to her feet.

"Look, you've done your buttons up wrong. On your dressing gown." The actress pointed out her mistake.

Before entering the room next door, the child knelt just at the threshold, placed both hands before her on the mats, and gave a polite greeting.

"Ah, come on in, come on in."

The old actor had an open script before him on a low, polished lacquer table. Removing his glasses from his large nose, he addressed the child impatiently.

With its shelf of tea things positioned near the entrance where the respectful apprentice sat, the rustic indigo cushions stacked in a corner ready for guests, the pot of orchids beside the makeup table, and other such refinements, the room had more style than her own, but was also more oppressive.

Even more oppressive was the presence of its owner, the old actor himself.

There it was, his distinctive smile, which she had known well from movie and TV screens and theater spotlights even before she moved into the dressing room next to his—only a single partition away—and trod the same stage. It was a perfect smile, both comical and sad, with all the lovableness of the clown.

But since that smile had begun to be directed at herself, the child had noticed something: while the rest of the face smiled both comically and sadly, the pair of large eyes was completely unmoved.

Now, too, his eyes, cold in an otherwise serenely smiling face, were
giving her a piercing look. The child replied with a beaming smile;
then, formally sitting as bidden in front of the old actor, she
endured his rigorous inspection.

The first time they'd met face-to-face in rehearsals, he had not
smiled at all. Those eyes had fitted into an aggressive, arrogant,
ill-tempered expression she'd never seen him wear on screen or in
the spotlight, and the child had shrunk in terror when they pierced her.

This had lasted no more than a second. To the child's formal "I'm
very pleased to meet you," the old actor had returned an unsmiling
glance and then bluntly turned his face away.

He had also been the only member of the cast who wouldn't agree
to rehearse lines with her. She had approached him timidly where
he sat—seeming to have chosen his seat expressly to avoid her—
and asked, "Please, Sensei, would you help me with my lines in Act
Two?"

The request had come out in an unexpectedly coy voice, and he
had said at once, "You don't need help. It looks as though you've
got it down pat." There was no way at all to approach him now. As
she turned dejectedly away, she was a little impressed, in a sneaking
sort of way. She was cross with herself for sounding so coy; she felt
she'd been a horrid child, and thought perhaps he'd seen through
her right from the start and known how horrid she was, and that
was why he'd taken that attitude. This thought aroused respect as
well as fear in her. He had stayed unapproachable for two days. But
on the third day, the moment he caught sight of her in the rehearsal
room, the old actor had called her name repeatedly. He was all smiles.
He drew her aside: "Look, here, I've got a nice surprise for you."

His tone and gestures could have come straight from the play.
Only his eyes, she noticed, were the same as the day before.
Chuckling with the pleasure of a shared secret, he had gotten the
child sitting up very straight in front of him. And then presented
his surprise, a big block of sweet bean jelly.

"Look, isn't that something? It's very good, this *yokan*. It's famous in fact."

The actor told her this in a confidential way as he unwrapped the block and sliced it himself with a knife his apprentice handed him. In the middle of the slicing he switched topics: "You know how fierce I looked yesterday? I was doing it on purpose."

The child was startled.

"Do you know why?"

Lowering her eyes to the old man's clumsy hands, she shook her head.

"I detest child actors, you see. They're repulsive."

The child raised her head and looked at the old actor's face. Though it still wore traces of a smile, his stern manner went oddly with the slicing of bean jelly.

"That's why I always look fierce."

His perfect smile lit up his face again.

"But I've been watching you, and you're different. You're not repulsive like the others. There you are, eat up."

Turning smilingly to her, he made the child pick up a thick slice of the jelly.

This was a disappointment. She had lost her fear of the old actor, and her respect. So he hadn't seen through her at all—he merely disliked child actors. And it was an added insult that he would deliberately treat her so coldly without even knowing what she herself was like, just because she was a child actor.

Something else had been bothering her, too.

The playwright had stopped the old actor on the way out of the rehearsal room and said, "What do you make of this girl? Interesting, isn't she? I've decided to give her my special attention. Haven't done that in a long time. I'm thinking of trying the two of you together in a comedy with a dash of pathos. I hope I can count on you."

The writer had his hand on the child's head. Without looking at her, the old actor said quickly, "That's a splendid idea," and hurried out. This had happened just the previous day.

Receiving the *yokan* with an expression of delight, the child had returned to her place near the exit and waited till the old actor's back was momentarily turned in order to press the gift on her mother. The child especially hated the sticky, sweet confection.

Since then, whenever he needed to deal with her, the old actor would produce the *yokan*. Having a sweet tooth himself, he was a believer in the efficacy of sweetness on the human heart, and the idea that a child could hate *yokan* seemed—unfortunately for her— never to enter his head.

From beneath the low lacquered table, once again he was bringing out a plate of the sweet slices. The child despaired. She realized, however, that as long as her host was convinced that the dark, gleaming jelly was a special treat she would at least have to take one; there was nothing else to be done. Sick at heart, she lifted a piece between thumb and forefinger, still hoping somehow to avoid having to eat it, but the old actor's eyes were on her. Finally the child opened her mouth and took a bite, in reality using only her front teeth to barely scrape the smooth surface. The shaving that slipped between her palate and tongue released exactly the sticky sweetness she'd imagined, and her spirits sank. The old actor nodded happily. Perhaps, thought the child, he knows I don't like *yokan*.

"You're a clever girl, so I probably don't need to tell you . . ." The old actor broached his subject with a formality that tried hard to pass as intimacy. The course of events was gradually, carefully taking shape in his head. The child could almost hear gears shifting minutely, and she tensed a little. Her own mind began to whir in a rush to anticipate what was coming.

"You know, a play isn't something we do on our own. No matter how good one actor might be, the balance among the members of the cast is terribly important. If the balance goes wrong, even when one individual is very good, the play won't be good as a whole. You do understand that, don't you?"

The child nodded firmly. The actor was bending forward at the waist and speaking with feeling.

"You're very good, but you still have a way to go in that respect. For example—"

He paused, looked up at the ceiling, blinked two or three times, then proceeded as if it had just come to him:

"Hmm. Take the end of Act One. You know—you and me and Chi are left onstage. Then Chi and I . . ." He ran rapidly through his dialogue with the female lead.

"At this point, because you've been eavesdropping, you become alarmed when you realize things have gone wrong."

Her alarm had raised a laugh since the opening night, but recently the child had added a little business of her own invention that had the audience roaring.

"That's not such a good idea."

The old actor regarded her with a slight smile as if to say he knew she was doing her best.

"Just think of the overall balance. Now that piece of dialogue, and especially Chi's delivery, is a very important part of the whole. So if you go distracting the audience—you see?"

At last the child understood the essence of the problem.

She'd received the same sort of talking-to over almost every scene. They were especially frequent where the scenes involved the female lead. The leading actress had never given the warning herself. Instead the message was passed on in one way or another by the director or a senior member of the cast, but it always came down to the same thing: never upstage the leading lady.

In some cases this warning was actually meant for the sake of the play. In others, as the backstage gossips knew well, it was to appease the leading lady. This prima donna, herself the personification of the term "theatrical child," viewed child actors with a furious jealousy and competitiveness that had already led to a number of incidents.

The child had no idea what was behind the warnings. She was too young to appreciate the balance of the play. She was also too young to recognize the pettiness and rivalry of someone who to her was a great star, who seldom spoke to her offstage, who would merely exchange a smile if their eyes happened to meet.

She therefore took the warnings to mean that she must never upstage the leading lady. She was quick to accept this as being the rule.

Yet the rule had a tendency to slip her mind completely the moment she was onstage. She was not in any sense a member of an ensemble. She gave no thought either to the supportive function of ensemble acting or to its opposite, the assertive self-consciousness found in any company.

Her gaze was fixed solely on the relationship between herself and the audience. What she liked about acting was, in truth, pulling the audience to her and pushing them away, caressing and hurting them, dragging them around and doing whatever she wanted with them. It was a cruel pleasure. An intensely cruel pleasure that had little regard for such niceties as the balance of the play or the subtle psychologies of her co-stars.

The child was seized by this pleasure the moment she had an audience in front of her, and promptly forgot the rule she had been taught again and again.

"I'm sure you understand, don't you? A clever girl like you."

Seeing the child agree, the actor relaxed.

"Yes, Sensei. Thank you," the child answered. She wanted to leave at once, but the stickiness of the *yokan* between her fingers prevented her. The old actor made no move to excuse her, but watched her steadily with half-bored eyes. Held captive by a single slice of *yokan* whose slippery surface bore two big front-tooth marks, the child shifted her weight awkwardly. The actor slowly responded:

"You've hardly touched it. Don't you like *yokan?*"

It was a rebuke, not a question. The child was as frightened as if she'd been caught misbehaving. Just when she'd resigned herself to there being no way out, a bell clanged. It was the thirty-minute call. The child ducked into the opening it provided. "Ah, I have to dress. Thank you, Sensei." And she nimbly made her escape from the heavy atmosphere.

"What did he want?" whispered the actress in their room next door. Placing the *yokan* upright on the edge of her table, the child simply reported the warning she'd received. The actress shrugged and looked around at the director.

"Old Chi's been kicking up a fuss again, I suppose."

Instead of replying directly, he commented, "I saw an amazing sight the other day."

He paused for effect. The actress leaned forward as expected.

"What? What happened?"

"At the end of Act One, I was going past Chi's room when I heard her yelling 'I've had it up to here with that child! *Do* something!' She was furious. I only caught a glimpse through the gap in the curtain, but it was his nibs next door who was stuck with the job of calming her down."

The actress nodded significantly. "Well," she said, "what do you expect from a woman who'd shove the kid aside onstage?"

"She what?"

"Didn't you know? It was ages ago. In that scene where we're all on together, Chi claimed our young friend here always got too far out in front, and she went"—here an emphatic jab with her elbow—"and knocked her aside."

"In front of the audience?"

"That's right. Maybe they couldn't see it, but we all could, and we were stunned."

"I hadn't heard."

"It's a famous story. Afterward the kid's mother was in tears, and there was all kinds of trouble. Wasn't there?"

The actress turned animatedly to look up at the child putting on her costume. The child only grinned.

What she'd experienced had not been so dramatic. She'd been standing onstage listening to the others' lines when there'd been a whisper in her ear: "Back, get back." It sounded like the leading lady who was then beside her, yet a furtive glance had revealed the woman facing in the direction she should be facing, her expression coolly in character.

Uncertain what to do, the child stayed where she was. Then, when the script called for the leading lady to take a step forward, her upstage elbow made a different gesture from the usual one and gave the child a prod. Caught off guard, the child retreated two or three steps.

She hadn't considered she'd been knocked aside, and it hadn't hurt a bit, so she didn't feel ill-used. She'd merely been taken aback. It had seemed more peculiar to her when two or three of the company—including her roommate—had reported it to her mother as a major incident and her mother had burst into tears.

It was beyond her why a prod from the leading lady should be considered such ill-treatment that it would make her mother cry. Being forced to eat nasty *yokan* seemed far worse to her.

There were so many things she didn't understand that she couldn't concern herself with every single one—only those that caused her real difficulties.

"Last spring, when she didn't like her role, they say she carried on and cried and threw up—did you hear about that?"

The actress and director were swapping stories of the leading lady's tantrums.

As she listened to these familiar episodes, the child's thoughts strayed to the leading lady's dressing room on the fourth floor.

Stepping into the small, square room—about half the size of her own—was like stepping inside a flame. From floor to ceiling all the walls were covered in rough-weave draperies of deep vermilion. The mirror stand, not the theater's but an elegant one she'd had brought in, was also bordered with a vermilion cloth rippling into gathers here and there. Every part of the decor was in burning colors—the cushions, the little table, the glasses, even the bottles of toilet water.

With the wall containing the window also covered under folds of drapes, the room's darkness was lit only by a lamp beside the mirror stand; this too was under a flame-red shade.

In the midst of the flame sat the leading lady, her back turned. She had on a fluffy pale pink gown and was involved in some activity by the light of the lamp. Both the old nannylike dresser and the chauffeur who doubled as a valet happened to have gone out and there was no one else about.

Standing still on the square of wooden floor just inside the door curtain, the child had watched the leading lady. She knew that she should say something, but her voice caught in her throat.

She was surprised at how much tinier the woman seemed here. A magnificent flame herself onstage, in this setting she was like a fragile petal trapped inside the flame.

The gossip about this woman that reached the child's ears was nearly all unkind. It told of her ruthlessness in going after the best parts, how she'd muscled others aside, how selfish and demanding she was.

But at the sight of the small, lone figure seated at the center of the flame, attending quietly to something, the gossip faded to a distant murmur like a running stream and the words "lonely princess" floated into the child's head. They played over and over to a simple tune.

Lonely, lonely princess. Lonely, lonely princess. She felt a sudden urge to hug her tight, as she would hug her rag doll.

In the mirror the leading lady looked up and let out a gasp. She claimed to be thirty-two, while others put the figure at thirty-eight, still others way past forty. She was single; there was also rumored to be a child of school age somewhere. But the dimpled face in the mirror was that of a startled little girl.

The child sheepishly held out a fancy square card she had brought on behalf of the caretaker of her apartment house, and asked for the star's autograph. "Come in," she said in her distinctive husky voice, and returned to her work.

Sitting behind her, the child peered over her shoulder and saw that she was drawing in a small sketchbook. Dipping a matchstick in black ink from time to time, she drew with deft strokes that slowly formed a portrait of the actress herself on the stage.

The child watched in admiration as the matchstick moved between those white fingers.

"See how well you can draw with a match?"

This was all she said, speaking half to herself, then fell silent. The child merely gave a faint nod and was silent, too.

Their faces, as the child leaned forward to watch her hand, were almost touching. She could have snuggled even closer, so close they would melt into each other. At this moment there was nothing to prevent her: neither the armor of the older actress's role—a chain mail of costume and makeup and technique—nor the invisible electromagnetic barrier that surrounds a great star.

Even that unpredictable adult mechanism had been disconnected for the moment.

The child felt a warm current of air brush against the downy hairs on her face. Though it was probably stirred by the ventilator, to the child it seemed a gentle breeze had wafted to her from the actress. She fancied another breeze, blowing from herself, was lightly ruffling the actress's hair. The scratching of the matchstick on the paper could be clearly heard.

She forgot completely that it was the leading lady who was breathing so close beside her, even forgot that it was an adult old enough to be her mother, in her happiness at having someone like herself there, gazing where she was gazing. Their eyes rested on the figure of the actress onstage, traced with a match. For some reason the drawing was her back view, so it, too, was gazing in the same direction.

When she reached a good stopping point, the actress sketched the same rear view on the child's card and signed it. Card in hand, the child left the room. They had barely exchanged a word. The encounter hadn't led to a special closeness, and she never went to the dressing room again, but that brief time spent inside the flame became a memory as precious as the pale gleaming pebble she had picked up in the playground in the rain.

After that, unkind gossip about the leading lady always made the child want to protest. She wanted to tell people they were all wrong. But having said that, she wouldn't have known how to make her case.

It wasn't that she wanted to insist the actress was really a nice person—she had no idea whether she was nice or not. Nor did she want to plead "Leave her alone, I like her." Indeed, it was always the people doing the gossiping for whom the child felt more fondness.

In the end, lacking the words to express what she'd understood in that brief shared time inside the flame, the child would always shrug the gossip off with a neutral expression.

The bell rang again, pausing once as if to catch its breath. It was the fifteen-minute call.

The child was ready. Wearing the patched dress that smelled freshly laundered and the cardigan that completed her costume, she clutched a broken-nosed clay doll from the prop department in one hand. The hem of her skirt that on opening night had hung well below her knees now half-covered her kneecaps.

"Well, have a good show."

The child drew herself up straight and went out. "Good show!" the adults said in chorus.

3

She went from room to room with her formal precurtain greetings, her wooden clogs—also from the prop department—making a muffled sound with their specially felt-covered soles. Day or night, the greeting among the theater people was always "Good morning." The child could shout this at any time of day with no hesitation, so perfectly was it suited to the actors' lives in which the raising of the curtain was the only dawn and any place not under stage lights was dark as night.

To the child, who felt she had a much firmer grip on the fantasy of the play than on the real world in all its strangeness and complexity, the words "good morning"—the words with which one wakes from a dream—were exactly right to announce that the performance was about to begin.

From the women's communal dressing room next door, she went downstairs to the men's communal on the mezzanine, then back upstairs to the third floor where she started with a room shared by three actors, then one shared by two actresses, and finally the private dressing room belonging to a rising young actress. She knocked and stuck her head in at the door to say "Good morning."

The scene that met her eyes gave off a strange light that burned it into her memory.

At the actress's side she saw the playwright. Atop the actress's favorite scarlet cushion, his stocky legs were swathed in soft cashmere trousers. His dark arms extended from the rolled-up sleeves of his dazzlingly white lawn shirt with its fine patterned weave. One hand rested lightly on his knee as he sat cross-legged, the other on his stomach, which was straining his buttons. The fingers looked very solid.

Behind him the actress's dresser, on her knees, had draped a towel over the playwright's shoulders and was massaging the iron-hard stiffness from them. Each time she pressed down, his head lolled.

The child took a step closer and was struck by the combined smells of expensive hair tonic from his well-groomed thinning hair and the eau de cologne with which he doused his body.

The impression that his cashmere trousers, white lawn shirt, and eau de cologne sought to create was immediately counteracted, however, by the jovial tufts of his eyebrows and the pebble-thick lenses of the glasses he wore.

The actress looked just as moist as the melon, a favorite delicacy of his, that was served with a spoon before him.

Though her features were not those of a beauty, at certain moments her small pointed chin, her large, widely spaced eyes, and above all her complexion, whose paleness seemed to rise from within, would make her a beauty of the highest order. She seemed able to choose these moments. She knew how to turn herself into one whenever she felt like it. This much the child understood, but the trick remained unexplained.

The actress was certainly making it work for her just now. She was very beautiful. Her body traced a flowing curve as, tucking her legs to one side, she extended her hand and dabbed the playwright's chin with a handkerchief.

Withdrawing the hand with no sign of haste, the actress turned her large eyes to the child and answered her charmingly. The playwright pushed the bridge of his glasses with a bent forefinger and gave a nod. "Ah," he said.

Sensing something dangerous in his elusive expression—he seemed neither angry nor particularly pleased—the child was about to take her head out of the doorway. But she was stopped by the playwright's voice: "Hey, there." As she ducked under the curtain again, the playwright directed a quick glance at her, his head wobbling in the dresser's hands, and summoned a smile. This made his eyebrows rise still further in the middle and gave him an extraordinarily amiable look. It was hard to believe he was the same man who flew into rages at rehearsals and thundered from the back of the theater.

The child was relieved: he must be in a good mood. Though she had never been shouted at herself, she knew how terrifying he could be in one of his quivering, stuttering rages, and had naturally been infected by the adults' wariness around him as they tried to gauge his state of mind.

When she came to think of it, the child noticed he'd never shouted at this young actress, either.

With a glance into space, not taking in any of their faces, the playwright said, "How's it going?" Having no idea how to set about answering, the child gave a little giggle with all the artlessness at her command. The actress watched her, completely at ease. The playwright went on wobbling.

Had he finished with her? Should she leave? Just as she began to be bewildered, the playwright asked, "Are you keeping up properly at school?"

The child's answer tumbled out. "Yes." The playwright was impassive still, as if he hadn't heard this reply, nor the actress's bland "Aren't you clever."

After a moment he said, "It's been two years now, hasn't it? In another two years you'll be ready for ingenue roles. If you stick at it."

"Yes, sir." The child laughed again, half in the actress's direction. The actress returned a meaningless laugh of her own. Again the child began to wonder whether to stay or go.

"Like a slice of melon, honey?" The actress spoke in a quite different tone now, not at all huskily. The child said, "No, thanks, I have to go," and slipped out of the door.

The awkwardness stayed with her all the way to the fourth floor.

People said that the famous playwright was especially fond of the child. This statement appeared whenever newspapers and magazines wrote about her. She was well aware that since arriving in Tokyo at his invitation she'd been following his advice on every move she made. Everyone was so envious of her, it was plain that such special attention from the playwright must make her a very lucky girl.

Yet when it came to what he actually thought of her, she was confused. He never stopped to talk to her, for example, as he did to her roommate and the other adults. He was always busy and rarely at the theater; when he did appear, he would whirl past her like a tornado, shaking off people who wanted him to tend to this and that.

Apart from when he directed her onstage, she could count on the fingers of one hand the times he had spoken to her. And even then, he spoke only of his hopes or advice for her future, and addressed these remarks more to her mother or the other adults present.

Still, on those few occasions, she'd been able to tell that the playwright was interested in her; at other times it was very hard to believe.

Unaware of the simple fact that to the writer—who always came straight to the point—she was a child actor first and last, she had taken literally the statement that he was fond of her, and was bewildered. In her confusion over whether or not he loved her, the child had failed even to understand why she was receiving such enviable attention—not knowing that roles continued offstage.

Still, the playwright's much-publicized fondness for her seemed a firmer link with the outside world than her other shadowy relationships. How to keep his supposed love weighed on her mind, and she couldn't help thrashing about, searching for clues. After each new awkward attempt, she was left just as confused.

Though the encounter in the young actress's room had been as awkward as all the others, the child sensed something different, something out of place. Today was the first time he'd called her back and spoken to her.

Yet the remarks seemed of no more importance than usual. She couldn't figure him out, and this terrified her—perhaps, she thought, this was why the adults feared him, too.

The beautiful young actress had astounded her by the way she acted toward this terrifying man, dabbing his chin like a naughty child's. How, she marveled, could anyone act like that? She had noticed long ago that the actresses seemed more at ease with him than the actors did, but this young star seemed to have some special knack.

The child's ignorance prevented her from making the obvious connection with recent rumors of an affair between the two. She simply felt faintly envious of the actress's way with the playwright, and wished that she, too, could learn the mysterious knack.

It had been a strange sight—the playwright sitting there letting her wipe his chin. In the tension of the moment she'd noticed only that he seemed somehow different from usual, but now, when she thought it over a little more calmly, she discovered why: he had looked funny. And then she hit upon something else.

He was embarrassed.

At this notion she grinned to herself. Not, of course, the sly grin of one who has caught a man philandering. It was a grin of delight. The child was delighted that the playwright had shared with her the glowing warmth of his embarrassment. That it was a secret between the two of them made it an even more precious gift. Perhaps he was fond of her after all, she decided.

The delight bubbled up from her swelling chest in bursts of song. Humming a tune between greetings, she went the round of the fourth-floor rooms.

In one of the doorways she came to another standstill. It was the dressing room of the actress who, for the past ten years or more, had been known as the playwright's "theater wife" and was treated accordingly. Ten years—her whole career, from her debut to the present day.

Shortly after he met the actress, the playwright had left his wife
and children and set up house with her. Although he could not
obtain a divorce, his legal wife was very seldom seen even on
formal occasions. The actress was his wife in all but name.

What can happen between a legally married couple in the course
of ten years or more had happened to them. The playwright was a
very ardent man. He had pursued one affair after another and left
the actress several times, always to return.

In all this time there'd never been a single rumor concerning
her—a fact that even the backstage scandalmongers found admirable. Her reputation as the woman who had stolen him from his wife
and children soon vanished, and in most people's eyes she became
the injured party.

No doubt they were moved to this new understanding by crude
pity for a woman who waits patiently for her man. The actress's
unpretentious nature, too, helped take the edge off people's sharp
tongues.

While many women in the company saw an affair with the writer
as their big chance of success, his "wife" was noticeably dedicated to
hard work. The older she got the more dedicated she became to her
craft, until she seemed to have no personal ambition at all.

Yet she was an easygoing woman, almost too easygoing. Adding
to this impression were her large build and her voice, a slow and
throaty contralto.

"Always cheerful, aren't you?" she said to the child, half-closing
her softly shining eyes to avoid the smoke from the cigarette
between her fingers. She spoke in the unaffected Osaka accent that
came naturally to her. The child switched effortlessly, too.

"Mmm. I'm young, that's why."

As always the actress's laugh was warmhearted. But the child felt
a cold, damp lump in her chest. On a nail in the wall hung a jacket
like the trousers she'd just seen the playwright wearing in the
younger actress's dressing room. A familiar necktie hung neatly

beside it. She felt a rush of guilt over the embarrassment the
playwright had secretly allowed her to see and the pleasure it had
given her.

"Would you like an orange juice?"

She didn't want one at all, but she nodded and perched on the
edge of the tatami. The child liked this woman, who neither conde-
scended nor teased. Her approach, as constant and simple as a blue
sky, made her one adult with whom the child could feel secure.

Once she sat down, she noticed a man's polished shoes on the
rack. She thought of the blue slippers neatly aligned in the entrance
to the young actress's room, where the playwright had left them
when he'd stepped onto the mats. There was a red pair of the same
type here. Sadness rose from the lump in her chest. Keeping her
eyes lowered, the child sucked on the straw in the orange juice that
the dresser brought her.

"How old are you, dear?"

"Eleven."

She raised her eyes and saw the actress pondering the word:
"Eleven, eh?" On the wall behind her was taped a sketch of the
playwright. The child had drawn it herself some time ago. When
she'd shown it to her, the actress had exclaimed over and over, "It's
so like him," and stuck it appreciatively to the wall. The face was
laughing, its eyebrows raised in the middle. With her lips pursed
around the straw, the child watched the woman's gaze grow distant.

There was a faint smile on the actress's face—a face of classic
proportions that suggested she had Western blood. She's pretty,
thought the child, but noted almost at the same time that her
freshness seemed to have dimmed. The child told herself again,
"She's pretty, this is real prettiness." But the recent memory of the
young actress's striking beauty had not left her.

The actress focused on the child again.

"Aren't you lucky? You have everything before you. You can do
anything you like."

She spoke with feeling, the smile still on her lips. The child was not at all sure what the woman was envying her for, but she felt the resignation in her voice like softly falling rain.

Clowning, she asked, "Will I ever be as beautiful as you?"

The woman's warm laugh set the child a little more at ease. But the fine rain continued to fall.

"Looks don't count. No matter how pretty you are, you'll get old. And there's no going back then."

As the actress's gaze grew distant again, she slowly raised her cigarette to her mouth.

The straw made a rattling sound in the glass. Setting it down, the child said, "Ah, that was good. Thank you," and stood up briskly as if to shake off fine drops of water.

"He will be out front tonight."

Seemingly unaware of the flustered reaction this produced in the child, the actress cast her eyes around, said "Ah," and picked up a new lace-bordered linen handkerchief that lay on the dressing table. "Would you give this to him? He always cries at his own plays. He went down to the production booth earlier—be a dear and go around that way, will you?"

The child accepted the errand and went out. Once outside, she hesitated. The actress had said, "to the production booth," but the playwright was in the dressing room of the pale-complexioned young actress on the third floor. There'd been no sign of him going past just now while she was drinking her orange juice.

But perhaps he had done so and she hadn't noticed, she thought, as she set off at a fast trot for the production booth, which was across the way from the office. She wasn't in any hurry to go back to that dressing room.

She pulled open a metal door and peered in. The booth, which projected out into the auditorium, contained only five empty seats, their backs toward her.

A bell rang three times: five minutes to go. She couldn't afford to wait around. She hurried back down the corridor lined with the stars' door-curtains, making as little noise as possible, and just as she was wondering whether to take the elevator—the lighted number "4" indicated it was already on its way up—its doors slowly opened.

The child stopped just in time. The playwright and the young actress were there. His "Don't you think so?" and her chuckle emerged ahead of them. Neither paid any attention to the child. The actress placed her hand lightly on the playwright's elbow and they passed by.

In a panic the child called out without thinking.

The two looked around, and for the first time the playwright's expression acknowledged he'd seen her. In one hand he gripped the folded handkerchief with which his chin had been dabbed. In spite of this the child thrust out the square of linen with which she'd been entrusted, blurted, "I was asked to give you this by—" and said the older actress's name.

With a sidelong glance and a "My," the young star swayed and squeezed his arm. He nodded, said, "Mmm," and shoved the linen handkerchief into his trousers pocket, already turning his back on the child.

The child hadn't time to dwell on the actress's beauty and the look the playwright had given her. Slipping past them and heading for the stage, she felt a tremendous sense of release. As she passed before the dressing-room door-curtains, she didn't even think of the actress with the distant gaze behind one, the actress trapped in the flame behind another. At the end of this corridor she would come out on the stage. That was everything now.

Half unconsciously greeting the stage manager and his crew, the rubber-sandaled prop man, the grips with hammers through their belts, and the costumed actors, the child headed for the stage.

Up ahead gaped the dark at the entrance passage to the wings. Not slowing her steps, she reached the darkness and climbed down into it, down the old wooden stairs.

The child submerged herself in the air and its mixture of paint, grease, dust, and mold. Through the darkness loomed floorboards pitted and pocked by clamps, lights trailing torn strips of colored cellophane, metal cables dully gleaming, the hem of a velvet blackout curtain. The darkness stretched away above and below, forward and backward, to right and left, proclaiming the vastness of the place.

Once in the wings, the child felt as though she, too, were expanding endlessly, becoming one with the dark. Tiptoeing down to the edge of the curtain, she stole a look at the house with the eyes of that vast darkness. Tiny people filled the rows. People who hadn't found their seats, people gazing around the theater, people reading their programs, folding their arms, laughing, talking, and all blithely unaware of what was about to happen.

Mouths opened and shut in all directions. Over there, and again over here, an arm bent and straightened. A torso flip-flopped, a back bent stiffly. A multitude of heads tilted backward, tipped forward, rotated, and jiggled loosely.

The child pressed her lips tightly together to suppress the laughter welling up inside her.

Already she could feel their responsiveness as they were drawn to her and pushed away, caressed and hurt, by her every word and gesture. Already she could feel the joy of manipulating countless threads—so difficult to handle, so easily tangled or snapped—pulled taut between herself and them.

The bell rang through the auditorium.

Taking a single deep breath, the child came out of the darkness and positioned herself onstage. Before her eyes was the dirty back of the curtain, an iron bar along its lower edge supported by a row of greasy cables.

A stagehand, having finished the final inspection, disappeared into the dark wings. The murmur of the audience faded, leaving a cough or two. The music began. Like a ship pulling away from the wharf, the entire outside world moved slowly away from the child. Becoming an idiot orphan who lived on the edge of town, she came slowly to rest in a solid world of plywood and paint and unbreakable glass and the sun of spotlights.

The child was no one but an idiot orphan, and could conceive of no world but this one. It was a nice day. Old memories and a clear awareness flickered in her blurred brain like sunlight through leaves. The child's face slackened and her front teeth showed between her open lips.

"Gosh, I'm hungry," she thought. "I haven't had anything to eat since yesterday. I wish I had something to eat. I wish I had a spoonful of sugar." This was the only certainty in her mind.

But she also sensed the presence of somebody watching the idiot orphan stand alone in this world. Somebody, somewhere, was watching intently. Watching with bated breath.

The curtain began to rise.

"Audience," whispered that somebody, "get ready to applaud."

THE
SOUND OF
WINGS

1

There are many tortuous alleys that lead off the main street between Tokyo's Shinanomachi and Yotsuya Sanchome. Some twist
and turn away, disappearing who knows where, some double back
on themselves to rejoin the same wide road, some are residential
and deadly quiet while others lined with tiny stores show vigorous
signs of life. In their old-fashioned way they each hold back in
obvious distaste from too much contact with the main road, as
if they still remembered the shock of the day when it sliced
through them destined to carry its uninterrupted flow of heavy
traffic.

On one of these alleys, in a house with an unimposing gate, lived
a woman called Tsuru and her husband. . . .

"Sensei."

[Note: The names "Tsuru" (crane) and "Tsu" are associated with a popular play
based on a folktale, in which a poor man who once rescued a crane marries a woman
who weaves priceless cloth for him on the condition that he must never look into the
room where she works all night. When she discovers that he has spied on her
weaving cloth from her own feathers, the crane bride flies away.]

Though they'd been married ten years, Tsuru still called her husband this. She couldn't break the habit of her student days, when he had been her teacher.

"Sensei." Tapping on the closed door of the study, Tsuru called again. "Come in" was the cheerful reply. Tsuru's hand hovered for a second, then made a natural movement to the knob, turned it, and pushed the door half open.

With the books arranged on their shelves like a halo behind him, Tsuyama was at his desk. Its large surface was covered by newspapers of many kinds. Perhaps in preparation for a critical study he had recently undertaken, he was sitting upright and snipping out articles with silver-colored scissors.

As she always did around her husband when he was working, Tsuru took care not to make a noise as she closed the door behind her and crossed the room to the imitation log fire. Keeping her back to her husband as she warmed herself before the gas flame, Tsuru listened to an inner voice urging her, "Go on! Get it over with now!"

"What is it?" her husband asked. That was enough to end her indecision. She turned quickly and let her first words fly out with the force of that action.

"There's something I want to discuss." Words she'd repeated to herself many times. Laying aside a clipping and the scissors and taking off the stylish reading glasses he'd begun wearing that autumn, Tsuyama answered good-humoredly, "What?" To her own astonishment Tsuru burst into tears. The words she'd prepared were clumsily distorted now, but she went ahead and blurted them out anyway.

"I've fallen in love with Toshi. And he loves me, too."

Tsuru sobbed. She held back the sobs to continue. "So, what . . . do you think . . . I should do?"

For a while the only sounds in the room were Tsuru's sobbing and sniffling mixed with the hiss from the gas flame. Tsuyama folded his hands under his chin. The sigh he let out seemed to thunder in Tsuru's ears. Yet his voice when he murmured "I knew it" was extremely gentle. She relaxed at once. Her sobs subsided and a sense of being set free, as if she were drifting off to sleep in some springtime meadow, made her body numb from the top of her head to the tips of her toes.

Tsuyama started to say something, stopped to clear his husky throat, then started his question all over again. It took time for its meaning to reach Tsuru, like a communication from a distant star. She nodded abruptly.

What he'd asked was "I suppose the relationship is already sexual?"

It was only after she'd nodded assent that Tsuru was struck by the strange new awareness of that fact. It's true, she thought, I've made love with Toshio. The realization was like having been turned inside out. Dazedly she was aware of herself struggling to turn the right side back out.

"Hmm." Tsuyama folded his arms and leaned back heavily in his chair. "Is that why he left?"

Toshio had been a boarder in the Tsuyama home; two days ago his suddenly announced departure had taken Tsuru herself by surprise. He'd explained to her as she had shakily followed him about while he efficiently packed his records and books and few clothes, "Surely you understand—I can't stay under Sensei's roof. I'll bet he's noticed. And I don't like this situation myself. In case things get ugly I don't want to be in the wrong any more than I have to be, don't you see?"

Toshio had left a message telling Tsuyama that he'd found a cheap apartment and was moving out; he realized this was very sudden but he would be back to express his thanks. Then he had driven off in a small rental car that had an angry growl.

Tsuyama forced a smile. "It got too uncomfortable for him here, did it?" Tsuru kept her eyes lowered. Her body was flushed, whether from the fire behind her or its own heat, she couldn't tell.

"And?" He paused as he did when prompting a student to think. "What do you want to do?"

"Don't know." New tears trickled down Tsuru's cheeks and she had another fit of sobbing. "I love you, too, Sensei. I don't know what to do." She could manage to say no more than this and it was nowhere near enough to convey what she really meant. Her feelings for Toshio had become an avalanche. For her husband she felt a deep affection like a calm in midocean and a respect that would never change. She would have liked to have kept hold of both, for each in his own way would be hard to let go. If, as she feared, this should prove impossible, she could only allow herself to be swept away by the avalanche.

That was what Tsuru really meant to say. But she couldn't bring herself to do so directly in front of her husband. It was not only the sobs that prevented her.

Abruptly, Tsuyama gave a laugh that had a sarcastic edge. "I wish I was broad-minded enough to condone your relationship."

Tsuru wiped her face over and over with the back of her hand. Tsuyama began to tidy up the papers scattered on his desk, and added, "If you can't part with Toshio, all that's left for us is divorce."

A profound loneliness swept through Tsuru. She raised her eyes. Her husband's meticulous gestures as he folded the newspapers one by one and piled them on a corner of the desk filled her with painfully fond memories. The brown cardigan he had on was one she'd made herself: it was looking decidedly shabby from constant wear. In the center of the desk was an ungainly teacup, the very first she had made, which now held a bunch of cleanly sharpened pencils.

The image of her husband entangled with her here sank beneath her tears, and then from their depths came a voice calling "Tsu." It was the nickname Tsuyama had given her when, ten years ago, he'd been a visiting lecturer at her college. The first time she was addressed in this way by a scholar for whom she felt a faint glow of admiration, Tsuru's heart had leaped with joy. She felt as though, like the white crane for which she'd been named, she was a small white creature whose delicacy had drawn his attention to her alone among all the young women in the class. Tsuyama seemed to be calling her to fly to him, and in answer she'd tried her wings.

"I haven't changed." Tsuyama was speaking as if reasoning with a very small child. "I love you, Tsu, and I always have. But if you've fallen in love with another man, then what can I do? You can't forget him, can you?"

Tsuru wept aloud. No matter how hard she tried to stop herself, the cries burst out with an energy that shattered her resistance. Why was the world such a sad place, she asked herself. After waiting patiently for her to quiet down, Tsuyama said laughingly, "Don't cry. It's me who should be crying." As Tsuru fought to catch her breath, she was filled with an immense gratitude and a sense of having done something for which she could never make amends.

"But what will Toshio do for a living? I can't imagine him supporting you."

"I . . . won't be living with him," Tsuru said hurriedly.

"You won't?"

"I can manage on my own. I'm not going to marry again, ever."

"Oh?" Tsuyama regarded Tsuru strangely, with a disbelieving, questioning look. Her decision had been made partly out of a sense of duty to her husband and partly in fear of falling into some similar situation if she were to live with a man again; since Tsuyama would have laughed at either of these reasons, Tsuru didn't elaborate.

"On your way to becoming the independent woman, are you?" As if taking back these teasing words, Tsuyama then added immediately, "Oh well, you should have a try at everything. You're still young."

Tsuru accepted this as sincerely meant and nodded emphatically.

"Now I'd like to ask a favor of you," he went on. "May I?"

Tsuru's eager look suggested there was no favor she could possibly refuse him.

"I may *sound* progressive, but when you come down to it I'm a forty-five-year-old man, and I'm lumbered with some old-fashioned ideas that I know on an intellectual level are absurd. But, still, I can't stand the thought of being a cheated husband."

Tsuru went rigid with shame.

"So the little favor I want to ask is this: don't make me look ridiculous to the world."

Tsuru was bewildered.

"No, I'm not talking about what's done already. There's no way to alter that. The fact is that you have already been unfaithful. What I want to know is whether or not you're prepared to make an effort to—shall we say—soothe my old-fashioned sense of honor which makes that fact so unbearable to me."

She still couldn't grasp what he meant.

"Suppose I were to ask you to break off all association with Toshio for, say, three months? Would you do that for me?"

Tsuyama looked searchingly into Tsuru's widening eyes.

"No one knows about your affair yet, do they?"

"No, of course not. I haven't even talked to my mother," she answered quickly. He nodded.

"That was wise. The thing is, if the two of you can stand just three months' separation, that should give me a chance to save face. Then we can get a divorce, and after that you're free to do as you please. If you'll agree to keep up appearances for my sake, you'll simply have to watch how you behave for a while. How about it?"

Tsuru swallowed hard. Before that rushing avalanche three days would have been penance enough. But three months? She could hear Toshio yell. Yet knowing what her husband must be going through, how could she deny him this? "All right," she said flatly.

"Are you sure? I said *all* association. There'd be no point otherwise. Think you can do it?"

When he pressed her like this she couldn't be sure, but she declared, "I'll do it. I'm not pretending that'll make everything right, but I promise I'll do it. I wouldn't want you to lose face, Sensei." She covered her own face with her hands.

"Thank you," Tsuyama said. She shook her head violently as if to ward off the awful weight of the words.

"Well, I've still got work to do, so why don't you go to bed, Tsu?"

Apologies, consolations, words of gratitude whirled inside her, but none found expression as Tsuru made sadly for the door.

"Toshio's a lucky man."

She started at this low murmur and turned to see her husband slowly stroking his left thumb along the blade of the silver scissors in his right hand. Hastily she averted her eyes and fled the study. Once outside she was overtaken by such exhaustion that she couldn't make it all the way to the bedroom, and for some time just stood there by the door.

2

Everyone, without exception, praised Tsuyama as a fine husband.

"He works hard and makes a good living. Being Mrs. Tsuyama must be an advantage wherever you go." Thus Tsuru was the envy of those who rated a husband by his status and finances.

"If I hadn't seen Mr. Tsuyama with my own eyes, I wouldn't have believed it—a married man who doesn't gamble, doesn't play around with other women, and doesn't stay out drinking half the night." Thus he also scored highly with those whose interest was in a husband's conduct.

"He's so dependable. They tell me he's a regular handyman—carpentry, electrical repairs, you name it—and he even cooks. For such an important man, he's not at all high-and-mighty. He's a real treasure." Thus Tsuyama also went over well with those who prized domesticity. Even the fact that there were no in-laws on his side to make his wife's life difficult was cited in his favor. But it was as an "understanding" husband that he attracted the greatest attention.

Tsuru didn't disagree with a single word of these praises. She would have liked to broadcast his fame as an understanding husband throughout the land. When, shortly after their marriage, she'd leaped up to stop him going into the kitchen and making them both a cup of tea, Tsuyama had said:

"Just because we're married it doesn't mean you have to turn into a traditional wife. I don't want someone to wait on me. I want a free, active woman who lives her own life. Can't we each treat the other as a free person? We have to get rid of the ridiculous old stereotype that it's the wife's job to make tea."

This had moved Tsuru, and shamed her, too. It wasn't as if she'd been uncritical of traditional marriage herself. Observing the married couple closest to her—her parents—she'd often thought her father's behavior wrongheaded or her mother's hopelessly docile. Surely that was the very reason she'd been attracted to someone like Tsuyama, who advocated a wider role for women in a new society.

Yet at the same time, deep down she had been resigned to leading a very ordinary life. This was not a considered decision but more a kind of instinct that told her she'd be safer that way. It was this instinct that had prompted her to behave toward men as a girl should, and again when she married, as a wife should.

In this almost instinctive way she had somehow ruled out the possibility of an ideal partnership. Tsuyama's words made her aware of this laziness on her part—for that was how she saw it. Laziness, and distrust of him. Ashamed and moved, Tsuru took his words to heart. And she began to learn all sorts of things in hopes of living up to his expectations.

Tsuyama had been very pleased. True to his word, he treated her always as a free individual, gave her books to read, took her to concerts and exhibitions, debated social issues with her, and helped her in various ways with her studies. To Tsuru he was more than an understanding husband, he was a teacher of life itself. It was small wonder that she still found herself calling him "Sensei."

For four years now Tsuru had been going to classes at a pottery studio; lately her pots had gone on display with her classmates' in a corner of a Shibuya department store and a trendy Harajuku boutique. The proceeds promised to give her a measure of financial independence. This, too, had been Tsuyama's idea. In line with his view that the woman of the future should develop a specific talent to ensure that she could always support herself, Tsuyama had urged Tsuru to get out more, as she was inclined to stay at home. As soon as she mentioned her interest in pottery, which she'd dabbled in at college, he found her a suitable studio.

Even his wife's confession of unfaithfulness hadn't shaken his high principles; he still recognized her freedom. A doubt did sometimes surface in her distracted mind: she knew very well without being told that there wasn't another husband as good and understanding as Tsuyama. So why . . . ?

She had no answer.

Her encounter with Toshio had had the effect of a window being flung open. She'd rushed toward him like a curtain in a gust of fresh air billowing out onto the breeze. Had Tsuyama, then, been as stuffy as a closed room? She'd never felt that. She'd always spoken her mind, always had her freedom.

With each reminder of how good and understanding her husband was and how grateful she must be, she had, however, been faintly aware of what seemed like another tiny drop falling into some deep place within her. As she was agreeing wholeheartedly with people's praises, the droplets would be falling, their echoes sounding a tiny protest. When she reflected on how lucky she was, when she smilingly acknowledged the compliments, the drops were steadily falling, falling. She could think of them only as drops; she had no idea what they were. She had a feeling they might have had something to do with the way she'd rushed toward Toshio, but she didn't pursue this line of thought.

Whatever thoughts she did pursue, in the end she dismissed them all as the flimsy excuses of a woman who had been unfaithful. Why she had done this to such a good and understanding husband was a question that, leaving only a guilty sigh, was quickly trampled underfoot and lost from sight in the wild dance of love.

3

The next morning, having slipped from the hold of a deathlike sleep, Tsuru woke with a sense of relief. Only the heaviness of her swollen eyelids reminded her of how the evening had ended, but like her body the memory had become lighter overnight. It would be more embarrassing than painful to face her husband now. However sorry she felt, the joy of having unburdened herself was still more intense.

But when she saw the other bed empty she sprang up in alarm. The silver scissors flashed to mind. Appalled at her carefree mood of a moment ago, Tsuru searched frantically: Tsuyama wasn't in the study, or the living room, or the bathroom. She half ran to the entrance hall and checked the rack there. A pair of his outdoor shoes had gone.

Had he simply gone out, or was there something more to it? As she returned uncertainly to the living room, she spotted a sheet of manuscript paper left on the table.

11 o'clock meeting. Didn't want to wake you as you were sound asleep. I'll be home for dinner. What's on the menu?

It was his usual message. Tsuru read and reread the casual lines, smiling in spite of herself. Their very casualness underscored

Tsuyama's thoughtfulness. Sensei really was a kind, generous man, she thought. Whether they were married or not, she must be good to him.

11 o'clock meeting. She checked the clock: it was a little after eleven. Counting off the hours till she had to start getting dinner, she reached for the phone. The number that Toshio had written down was firmly fixed in her memory. He was sharing a student friend's apartment.

When someone answered, she caught herself lowering her voice to ask furtively for Toshio—and then she went and added, before she was asked, "I'm his sister."

I'm his sister. As she waited for Toshio to come to the phone, Tsuru, her hand over the mouthpiece, groaned. "Just listen to me." The line could have been taken straight from some daytime soap opera.

"What's up?" It was Toshio's energetic voice. It gave Tsuru such a lift that her heels in the slippers she was wearing actually rose off the floor.

"Toshi, I told Sensei last night."

"You did? Bravo."

Even at a time like this, Toshio's reaction was as startlingly simple as a child's drawing of the sun, as upbeat as a festival in a hot country. The surprise it gave her was a pleasant one, of course; she very nearly laughed out loud.

"And was it okay? Are you all right?"

"Me?"

"I mean, he didn't hit you or anything?"

"Don't be silly. Sensei wouldn't do a thing like that."

Tsuru was rather offended on Tsuyama's behalf.

"No, I didn't think so, but I couldn't help worrying. There's no telling what I'd do in his place."

"Sensei isn't a roughneck like you, Toshi."

"So how'd it turn out?"

"We're getting a divorce."

"Ah. That's wonderful. Sensei is a very decent man, isn't he? I'll have to tell him so properly, in person. Now you'll come right over, won't you? Want me to come and meet you somewhere?"

"It's not as easy as that."

She couldn't do it over the phone after all, she'd have to meet him: thus Tsuru converted her unthinking desire to see him into a necessity. If she were to keep her promise to her husband, it was necessary to have everything arranged today. She also had misgivings about Toshio's end of all this; she would have to make him a solemn promise, face-to-face, to see him again.

When she offered to meet him and explain, Toshio was simply delighted. As she wavered, he suggested, "How about The Gendarme?"

This was a coffee shop in Yotsuya run by a woman friend of Tsuru's. Now that was being *too* relaxed, she thought. A little impatiently, she said, "Oh no. I don't want anyone to know yet. Not even Kanako. We'd better go somewhere quieter."

"Then why not come here?"

"But what about your roommate?"

"Oh, don't worry about him. We can tell him to go out."

Tsuru was curious to see where Toshio would be living, and glad of the privacy they would have together before so long a parting.

"Okay, then," she said.

"I'll meet you at the station."

"Well . . ." Having gone this far she now felt guilty about walking from the station at Toshio's side. "Don't worry. I'll follow the map you gave me with your phone number."

"It's not easy to find."

"I'll do it. Don't worry."

"Well, call if you're lost."

Toshio spoke as if it were she who was younger. She must seem pretty unreliable, Tsuru thought with a wry smile.

"I can't wait," he added. "I know it's only been a couple of days, but I can't seem to concentrate on anything. I've got to see you."

Toshio's confiding tones lingered in Tsuru's ear after she'd put down the receiver, bringing back exactly the way he looked and the touch of his hand on her cheek. She felt a tremor.

There was no time to waste deciding what to wear; she hurriedly put on a short coat over her sweater and slacks, stuffed the map and her purse into her pocket, and left the house. Emerging from the narrow street, where cars had left scratches like brush marks on the telephone poles and the corners of concrete block walls, she followed the main stream of traffic till she came to Shinanomachi Station, where she took the train for Nakano.

As he'd said, the place was hard to find. Small streets resembling the one on the map crisscrossed confusingly, and there were whole blocks of buildings any of which could have been the right one. After retracing her steps several times along the same street, Tsuru stopped at the entrance of the alley that seemed the most likely, and peered in uncertainly at a two-story rectangular mortar building.

Under its slate roof the no-nonsense exterior was relieved only by a row of three square windows upstairs, but the two narrow concrete steps at the entrance were bordered by overcrowded beds of sweet daphne and rhodeas and laurel bushes, while one branch of a persimmon tree leaned over the wooden fence that almost hid the first-floor windows, as if to take a closer look at the brightly colored child-sized bicycle that was parked out in front, its wheel angled in to the fence.

This seemed to be the place, but she couldn't reconcile herself at first to the idea that Toshio was in there, in a setting that must always have existed quite independently of herself. Flexing and unflexing her fingers in her pocket, Tsuru stood gazing up at the building for some time.

The door rattled open and a young man came down the steps, a cigarette in his mouth. Before Tsuru could back out of the way, he caught sight of her and said, "Ah," as he took the cigarette from his mouth, then pointed behind him with the fingers that held it and added curtly, "This is it. Second floor, down the end," and brushed past her.

Tsuru recognized him. He was the man they'd run into at a Tadanori Yoko poster exhibition that Toshio had taken her to. He'd introduced him as a friend. So it must be his apartment, Tsuru concluded as she reached for the door that he'd just closed. Though he'd come and gone before she'd had a chance to collect her wits and greet him, she was reassured to find that this setting had not been entirely unrelated to herself, and she stepped inside without further hesitation.

There was a black telephone at the foot of the stairs. Tsuru could readily imagine the tall figure of Toshio leaning against the wall, one leg bent double and the receiver in his hand. And now there he was: the sound of Pollini playing a Chopin prelude from behind the far door signaled Toshio's waiting embrace.

But she was wrong. Toshio didn't throw his arms around her and greet her with a kiss. He was wrapped in the piano music, gazing morosely at his feet thrust out in front of him. The look he gave her when he raised his eyes held a sullenness she'd never seen before.

"It's lovely and warm in here."

Across the distance she'd been unable to cancel with a hug, Tsuru spoke up. The room was in fact very warm and reeking of kerosene. She stood just inside the door, uncomfortable in the atmosphere that was not only close but permeated more by the other man's presence than by Toshio's, until finally he slapped the cushion he'd been sitting on and pushed it in her direction. "Here. You'll need this, the tatami's dirty. Not that the cushion's much cleaner."

This was her funny old Toshio who couldn't stay serious even in the middle of a sulk.

"What did you want to tell me?" he asked sternly. Taking off her coat and sitting formally on the cushion, Tsuru broke the news of her promise to her husband, putting it as positively as she could. Toshio listened glumly without helping her out or even nodding.

"I thought it might be something like that," he said when she'd more or less finished. His tone was bleak. "I was right, then. Sensei means to drive us apart."

This was an interpretation that had never crossed Tsuru's mind. "But he's going to give me a divorce," she protested.

"Then why wait? If he genuinely meant to set you free, he wouldn't want to go on living with you a moment longer. With a woman who's in love with another man? I wouldn't, if it were me."

"But I told you: he says it's a matter of honor. He says that in spite of understanding on an intellectual level he still can't bear being exposed as a cheated husband, and so he's asking us at least to keep up appearances."

"That's bullshit. It's absurd. Think about it, Tsu." His morose manner gone now, Toshio leaned forward urgently, his eyes intent on hers. The fierce look in them scared her.

"It'd make the break look more natural if the two of you were to live apart for a time, but that's not what he wants, he wants you with him, and everything as it was. What he's actually doing is separating you and me. Don't you see?"

Tsuru felt the pull of Toshio's persuasion and braced herself, fighting to keep her balance.

"But in just three months from now—"

"Three months or two, what difference does it make? There's no telling what'll happen in that time. That's what Sensei is counting on. I'll bet he has no intention of ever letting you go, Tsu. He's dreamed up this weird condition to give himself time to try and get you back. It's obvious."

The way her husband had acted the night before came back to her. His calm acceptance of an announcement that would have made most men lose their heads, and his willingness to recognize her freedom. His request, made without the slightest hint of coercion, even a little sheepishly. His stroking the blade of the silver scissors and murmuring "Toshio's a lucky man."

She didn't much like the contrast with the way Toshio was acting, seeking out Tsuyama's hidden motives so belligerently, even if it were from the strength of his desire to have her for himself. It must have been this combative mood that put such twisted suspicions in his head. Tsuru said firmly, "Sensei isn't like that. He's just not that kind of person."

"I know. He's a fine, decent man. But—"

"You don't understand, Toshi. You couldn't make an accusation like that if you did."

"I'm not so sure. . . ."

Taken aback by her firmness, Toshio let his sentence trail off. The record had ended unnoticed, and the tread of slippered feet could be heard downstairs. Tsuru realized she'd raised her voice. She quieted down.

"Toshi, never mind his reasons. Don't you think we owe him that much? Compared to what he's giving up for us, what does three months' separation matter? If he thinks he can drive us apart so easily, then I'm going to prove him wrong."

"Such heroism. It's a bit worrying, this stoic tendency of yours." But Toshio's objections had lost their force.

"I hate to have to do this to him, Toshi. He's such a decent man. If there's anything I can do to save his feelings, I want to do it."

"I wouldn't hurt him deliberately, either."

"Then hold off for three months. It's not important. In the end it's for me to choose who I spend my life with and I've chosen you. Nothing anyone says will make me change my mind. We could be separated for years and it wouldn't matter. Don't you trust me?"

"I trust you. All right. We'll do as you say."

Toshio was gazing at Tsuru with an ardent tenderness that revealed him completely. When she put her arms around his neck and kissed him, his whole body responded at once.

"I must be out of my mind," he began. He was holding her tightly in his arms, his jaw bumping her head as he spoke. "It's bad enough not seeing you even for a short time—I can't think of anything but you. And knowing you and Sensei are living together, just the two of you under one roof, is more than I can stand. My imagination runs away with me."

Unable to reply, Tsuru let out a laugh that could have meant anything.

"I'll never last three months this way," he went on. "I've got to get a job and work so hard I won't have time to think. We'll need the money, too, when it comes to moving in together."

It wasn't time yet, she decided, to tell him she was going to live alone. That would have to wait until they saw each other again. She didn't want another argument with Toshio today.

"Know what I'm going to do first?" he asked.

"What?"

"Go right out and buy the *Vacation Job News*."

Tsuru burst out laughing. "Is that the only source of jobs you know?"

"Uh huh. I'm not too well up on things like that. And another thing—" As Toshio's stroking hands descended from Tsuru's hair and made their way up under her sweater, what had been smoldering in her grew. "I'll need to go on a vegetarian diet. Three months—how'm I going to make it?"

It was all she could do to break herself free from his tightening arms and prevent a fire igniting inside her.

"Not today."

"Wha—?"

"It would seem as if that's why I came here."

"You can't be serious!" Toshio cried, sounding almost tearful. "I'm not going to be able to touch you for three months! How can we let a chance like this go?"

Tsuru slipped her arms into her coat. "If we can't control ourselves today, how will we make it through the next three months?"

"You don't want to make love?"

"I feel the same as you."

"Then why not? We can be on our best behavior starting tomorrow. I'm about to explode."

Tsuru looked frankly at him. "I'm afraid I might go to pieces if we did. I don't trust myself."

"So what if you did? Love never was neat and tidy."

"No, I want to do this the right way."

"You're such a goddamn stoic. I can't stand it."

Toshio threw himself backward, banging his head hard on the windowsill.

Tsuru took the train to Shinjuku, shopped in the Odakyu's basement food section, and went home to cook Tsuyama a special meal.

Arriving just as it was ready, Tsuyama chatted over dinner as if nothing had happened the night before. He was so relaxed that the evening seemed almost an anticlimax.

That night, however, Tsuru was bewildered when he came to her bed. Her first impulse was to turn away, but she couldn't justify doing that. She had set herself to soothe his injured sense of honor, which meant she could never speak of what had happened with Toshio, nor even hint at it. But what other reason could she possibly have? To say she didn't feel like it seemed callous after last night.

Besides, she thought as she gave way, it wasn't as if she'd stopped sleeping with her husband after the affair with Toshio began, so there was no sense in having scruples now. Her love for Tsuyama might no longer be sexual, but for the time being they were still husband and wife.

Although she had had to overcome the urge to refuse him, the act that followed was the same as always.

But this Tsuyama who wanted a woman's body when he'd just learned of her feelings for another man was a stranger to her; she couldn't help finding his actions somehow chilling. And they seemed to have taken on a different kind of intensity that wasn't like her husband.

In the dark she saw Toshio cry, "You're such a goddamn stoic. I can't stand it," and bang his head on the windowsill, and she wished they had made love after all.

4

In November of the previous year Tsuyama had gone to a concert of contemporary music. As he smoked a cigarette in the lobby during intermission, he noticed a tall young man in threadbare jeans sneaking glances in his direction between sips from a paper cup. The young man moved from the periphery to stand in front of Tsuyama and say, "I read your article in last night's paper." Though a layman, Tsuyama occasionally reviewed concerts or records; the piece referred to had dealt mercilessly with a foreign pianist who regularly sold out his recitals in Japan and carried off both the critics' accolades and a tidy sum of money.

"I've always thought he was third-rate, so I got a kick out of your review."

Tsuyama's pleasant reply seemed to genuinely delight the young man, who then sought his opinions on other musical matters, offering his own ideas in return with the joy of one who has found a fellow heretic. His ideas had substance enough to hold Tsuyama's interest.

"I'd have taken your course in civil engineering if I'd thought you'd always talk about music."

"Oh, you're one of our students?"

"Yes, every now and then. I'm Toshio Kotani."

"What's your department?"

"Economics."

"What year?"

"I'm in my fifth, and most likely heading for a sixth. It's a hard life. But not too hard."

The bell was ringing. It was Toshio who asked what Tsuyama was doing after the concert, and Tsuyama who suggested a cup of coffee.

Toshio knew Tsuyama's work well. He followed social commentary and cultural theories more avidly than he did his own field, and could be called an admirer of Tsuyama's. Tsuyama felt an agreeable recognition that this respectful young man's perceptions fell into line with his own considered thought. Though Tsuyama himself had by far the greater store of knowledge and experience, Toshio had new knowledge that lay out of his reach, contemporary experience that only youth could claim, and a painfully sharp sensibility whose jabs had a stimulating effect on Tsuyama, reviving a part of him that had begun to calcify.

Neither of them tired of their conversation in the least, each sensing a pleasing degree of attention in the other as they expounded their ideas, now agreeing, now differing. From the coffee shop, via a Shinjuku jazz spot that Toshio knew and a Shibuya sushi bar that Tsuyama knew, they finally arrived at Tsuyama's house after one o'clock in a pleasurably drunken state. They then sampled Tsuyama's record collection almost till dawn, brushing aside Tsuru's fears of complaints from the neighbors.

From that day on Toshio had been a frequent visitor.

As one who knew Tsuyama well, she could understand her husband's respect for Toshio; as a pupil of her husband, she appreciated Toshio's admiration for him. She grew to feel a dual affection for the young man—in part shared with her husband, and in part her own.

After an initial polite reserve toward Tsuru, Toshio quickly began to feel at home. Their attitude to Tsuyama gave them the kind of rapport that two school friends or a brother and sister might have. The sides of the triangle thus completed were intricately interlocked.

"It would save a lot of trouble if I just moved in with you," Toshio had said jokingly at breakfast one morning. As they entered the New Year, he was spending an increasing amount of time with the Tsuyamas. The three went to the theater and on a tour of the winter sights of Kyoto. Toshio had once again missed his last train home to Asakusa (where his parents ran a liquor store with the help of his brother and his brother's wife) and had ended up staying the night.

"Why don't you?" said Tsuru. "You can be our servant."

"That's no way to treat a future prime minister."

"Oh, I thought you were going to be a great poet."

"No, there's more money in being prime minister."

"You wouldn't last three days. Prime ministers have to work, you know."

"Uh oh. Maybe I'll stick to poetry."

"Make up your mind. Even poetry takes work, you know."

"It does? Damn. There must be some way I can make an easy living."

"You're doing it already."

"This isn't as easy as it looks. When I get home my Mom and Dad will start in on me about helping in the store, and my brother and his wife always insist I pay board, and you can't get a decent part-time job these days. If I fail this year's exams and have to repeat, the whole family will be after me, I can tell you. I'd walk out if I could, but I can't afford it. It's rent-free at home, and you can't beat that. So there I am. Trapped."

"If your ideal in life is not to work at anything, you will always be trapped."

"That's not my true ideal."

"Oh? What is?"

"I'll confess if you promise not to laugh."

"Go on, I won't laugh."

"To do something worthwhile."

Tsuru roared with laughter.

"I mean it. I was hoping you wouldn't laugh. But I'm not getting anywhere because I can't work out what is worthwhile. It's a big mystery to me."

"Would you really like to move in with us, Toshi?" Tsuyama said. They both looked at him at once. "You could, you know, if you wanted to. The six-mat tatami room is empty. In return, since I'm sure you wouldn't want to take advantage, how would it be if you helped me in my work? I've been thinking of getting someone in to file my papers and so on. Though I can only pay you pocket money."

That evening Toshio had come to live with them. Though he described himself as lazy, when so inclined he could be efficient and attentive to details; he was even happy to assist with the housework or shopping from time to time.

While Tsuru had never found life with her husband lacking, with the addition of Toshio it was better than ever. She enjoyed every day. Her picture of herself seemed to be changing from a monochrome to many colors.

Though their affair had shaded the scene with fear, as long as she and Toshio kept this new coloring well hidden their daily round went on, happily unchanging. While telling herself uneasily that it couldn't continue, she hoped it would last forever. Her affection for her husband, her passionate love for Toshio, her friendship for them both lived compatibly inside her creating a unified beauty like a woman's healthy body. And she wanted to keep that beauty alive.

But the triangle had come apart with Toshio's leaving. By moving away he had tacitly forced a decision on Tsuru and gambled on her choice.

Faced with the loss of Toshio, she had plunged Tsuyama into a dilemma by her confession and had robbed him of both wife and friend. From Toshio she had taken away the teacher he revered, and for this, too, Tsuru blamed herself. But sometimes she would see these things in a different light.

If Toshio hadn't left she would never have confessed of her own free will. Their ménage would have lasted as long as her husband had allowed it. It was Toshio and her husband who had not permitted life to be the beautiful thing that she had conceived. The two of them had cut its life short.

It was a selfish thought, she knew, but she missed that beauty all the same.

5

Having firmly warned Toshio against coming to the studio or house, writing, or phoning, Tsuru was disconcerted when she caught herself frequently hoping for some sort of contact. When the doorbell rang at the back door, she'd think, "Could it be—?" though it was bound to be the dry cleaning, and at the sight of the deliveryman's face peering around the furtively opened door, she would feel distinctly disappointed. She would pick up the day's mail and be half afraid to look in case there was a rare letter for her, probably sent under a false female name or some such ruse to escape her husband's notice. And the ringing of the telephone always thrilled harshly inside her.

After several letdowns that were like blows to the stomach, she was able to give up these hopes and, on the third day after their temporary farewell, prepare herself at last to endure the separation.

She decided to stop counting the days. It only increased her desire to see him, and each day that was spent with her eyes on a point three months hence dragged by unhelpfully. If she kept her mind on what was immediately in hand and turned her back on the coming months, a single day would pass with surprisingly little resistance.

They were empty days all the same, but there was nothing Tsuru could do that would fill their hollow, frothy, drafty spaces. She became afraid of having spare time in which she would take stock and count the days in spite of herself.

She kept mind and body fully occupied. She grew passionately involved in her pottery; creative work could absorb an unlimited amount of thought and labor. And there was also the more practical incentive of having, sooner or later, to make her own living.

The time she spent in Tsuyama's company, which must once have been a pleasure, she would now have gladly avoided. He continued to behave as if nothing had happened, but Tsuru couldn't do the same. She would imagine what Toshio might have said at a particular point in the conversation, or worry while looking after Tsuyama over how Toshio was managing. Feeling insufficient once more toward Tsuyama, she always wore herself out in the end.

On the seventh day after the parting, Tsuru had got her husband off to work and was musing, as she washed the breakfast dishes, on the limits of what a potter could do. When she took a lump of clay in her hands she wanted to mold it into everything under the sun. Not just pots and figurines but trees and flowers and houses, pebbles and stars and water, chopsticks and pencils and shoes.

There was a limit, however, to these objects' usefulness. Nobody wore pottery shoes or wrote with clay pencils. Not having the desire or the confidence to become an artist, she had applied her ideas to brooches and tableware that seemed to be proving unexpectedly popular with younger customers; but still she wasn't satisfied. She wanted to make not shoelike ashtrays and vegetable-shaped trinkets but actual shoes and vegetables.

Perhaps, as potters had done over the ages, she ought to be concentrating on making practical utensils. What was the point in making something utterly useless just to please herself? But what—she heard herself echoing Toshio—did it mean to be useful? . . .

The phone rang. Tsuru was still lost in thought as she went into the living room and picked up the receiver. "Hello. The Tsuyama residence."

There was no reply but the caller's breathing in her ear. She was fairly sure who it was.

"Hello. Tsuyama here."

"Hi, Tsu."

"Toshi!"

At the sound of that familiar voice all her hard-won self-control collapsed and a scalding hot-blooded impatience rose through her body.

"What's happened?" Joy had overcome the reproachful tone she'd intended. But she stuck with the reproach: "I thought I told you not to phone."

"Come on, now, Tsu, I've stood this for a whole week. Don't be like that." The unhappiness in his voice made it all the more affecting.

"You're impossible." Her tone let him know that he was forgiven already.

At once he perked up. "I'm glad we can talk. Now I won't go crazy—I think."

"You really are impossible, Toshi. You mustn't give up now."

"But what's the point? I've had it. You feel the same way, don't you? Why not admit you're dying to see me?"

"Yes, of course I am, but . . ."

She'd have a hard time reasoning with him, she knew.

"I'm starting to see red. We're lovers, we're in love, it's only natural to want to hear your voice and see your face. There's nothing wrong in that. What, I've been asking myself, is the point of suffering like this?"

The question was not lost on Tsuru. Yet she could hardly admit that he was right; she was too entangled for that.

"You know what I mean, don't you, Tsu? And all on account of Sensei's pride. Pride! What's that matter beside the fact that we love each other? I can't believe it's worth going through this torture."

These were her own suppressed doubts that he was dragging into the open one by one. Though it made her uneasy, it also gave her a certain satisfaction.

"Toshi, it *is* necessary. Remember I want to make the break with Sensei as painless as possible."

"That's dishonest." This time he'd touched a vulnerable spot. "We've cheated Sensei already in every way you can think of."

Tsuru saw his point: it was dishonest to want to part painlessly after all that had gone before. Perhaps her wish to save face for her husband was also, in the end, a self-serving need to disguise the fact that she had hurt him. Perhaps sheer self-interest had figured too: if she were to walk out on him too recklessly she might have problems at the studio where he had introduced her and where her future was already precarious enough.

Yet the desire to somehow meet her husband's wishes was not altogether false, either. She was at a loss for words.

"So how about it? Forget that stoic bit," Toshio said. "If the important thing is saving face, it won't matter whether you and I are actually in touch—all that matters is that he believes we're not."

To Tsuru, who was finding the separation as hard as Toshio was, this argument had great appeal.

"I suppose so. We've deceived him before. I guess it's too late to turn honest now." She spoke with a kind of resignation, reconciling herself to losing the mask of decency she'd constructed out of nothing more than good nature. And then she found she didn't mind its loss as much as she'd thought. She went on to declare, this time with a sense of finding her feet on solid ground after desperately treading water off a rocky shore that had not been as distant as it appeared, "But, Toshi, we mustn't meet."

"Why not?"

"I couldn't face Sensei. Telephoning is enough. Okay?"

"I can't see any difference."

"I can."

"Okay, okay. It'll do. Just to hear your voice is progress."

As his own voice boomed happily, Tsuru suddenly thought of his lodgings and asked, "Is it safe to phone from there? You won't be overheard?"

Toshio was entirely unconcerned. "Of course not. Wouldn't care if I was."

"But you will be careful? If Sensei were to find out he'd be more hurt than ever. We must make absolutely certain he never does."

"Sure. Then to be on the safe side I won't call you. You call me."

"When should I call?"

"Whenever you can. As often as you can. I'm usually here."

"How can you be, with classes and a job to go to?"

"It's no good. Over the past week I found I was spending most of the time worrying about you. I can't get a thing done, and I'm not going to fight it."

That he could lose his heart so frankly was exhilarating. That it was to herself he'd lost it was an almost insupportable joy. Yet she fretted that he'd never get anywhere in the world if he carried on like this; he couldn't stay a student forever. While she loved him for his way of doing precisely as he pleased, she worried that this freedom was dangerous in a lover. On the whole the worry gave way to the love. Tsuru breathed into the receiver.

"Anyway," Toshio continued, "don't worry, I'll settle down in a little while. I'm thinking actually of getting my old job back, loading trucks." Suddenly mischievous, he added, "Physical fatigue, that's what I need. The vegetarian diet isn't doing a thing for me. Tsu, Tsu, I want you."

He whispered the last words; Tsuru received them as a caress.

6

Like the image in a distorting mirror, appearances change depending on where a person stands. Time and one's own decisions change where one stands. When Toshio suggested that he'd been in love with her from the first moment they met, reminding her of various things that had happened between them to prove it, Tsuru could also come up with evidence that she had loved him. She could now see how this thought and that feeling, this word and that gesture, had arisen from her love for Toshio. The events of that night had been meant to happen, she reflected.

A doubt remained in Tsuru's mind, however: perhaps they might never have embarked on their affair if it hadn't been for that one night.

Toshio had been living in the Tsuyama household for a little over a month when they had first become lovers. It happened the first time that Tsuyama, on an overnight research trip, had left them alone together.

Having seen him off at the station that morning, Tsuru had gone to the studio and Toshio, for once, had gone to the university. Tsuru came home a little later that night than Toshio.

As Toshio had been busy that evening and had said he would eat out, Tsuru had taken the opportunity to go with a group from the studio to see an exhibition of Mashiko ware in the Ginza, then had invited her friend Kanako from The Gendarme out for a leisurely meal; she was thus unusually late coming home.

There were no lights on in the house, but Toshio's worn-out sneakers had been discarded in the hall. Thinking this odd, Tsuru slipped quietly into the living room and there found Toshio, his back view silhouetted in the light of the streetlamps as he leaned against the sill of the open window and gazed out. Tsuru watched him for a moment before she reached for the light switch.

"Oh, you startled me, Toshi. I didn't see you there." Delicacy made her shrink from letting him know that she'd seen him lost in a world of his own, in the darkness and the cold.

Turning with a somewhat exaggerated blinking of his eyes into the suddenly bright room, Toshio said, "Oh, you're back." Then he shifted himself listlessly to the sofa. The mood that the bright light should have dispelled was still plainly evident in his voice, the way he moved, his expression. Tsuru went on pretending not to notice.

"You haven't even put the heater on. There'll be icicles hanging from the ceiling."

She bustled about closing the window and lighting the heater before Toshio could get up. Next she offered, "Like a cup of tea? I've bought a cake."

She couldn't see anything else that needed doing.

"No, don't bother. I've had a drink or two," Toshio answered, raising his eyes but not far enough for their gaze to reach her.

"You can have the bath if you want it."

"No, it's okay. I took one yesterday."

"You mean the day before. Toshi, you're a grub." Tsuru laughed and began to take the cake away. This was by no means the first time she and Toshio had been alone in the house. On each occasion Tsuru had found him more reserved and distant than usual. She had even wondered whether it was only Sensei he wanted to know better, whether he was oblivious to her existence. But this thought was always banished by the friendly interest that Toshio showed when he helped her around the house or listened attentively or told her about himself.

It had occurred to Tsuru that such aloofness can indicate all too close an interest. But she wasn't prepared to apply this knowledge. She was seven years older than Toshio and not especially beautiful; it couldn't be that Toshio—who could surely attract any number of girls—had taken a special interest in her. It was ridiculous of her to entertain the idea for a moment, Tsuru thought, and she took great pains to keep away from it.

Having avoided the right answer all along, her inquiries into the mystery naturally went around in circles. As she put away the cake, Tsuru wondered again at Toshio's reserve. Growing a little impatient, she was tempted to shake the answer out of him.

"Well, time to turn in, I guess." Toshio's voice was muffled as he stretched. Tsuru had already said automatically, "Oh, it's not that late," when she became aware of a reluctance to simply let him go. And Toshio himself gave no sign of departing.

"Do you have to be up early?" she asked.

"Not really." The evasive reply drove her a step further toward shaking him.

"Then won't you stay for a drink?"

Toshio looked her in the face for the first time. "Good idea. But not by myself."

"I'll join you."

"I thought you didn't drink."

"Never mind, I was just thinking I could do with one. Something not too strong."

"Good for you. I'll get it."

Whatever it was that Toshio had been wrapped in fell lightly away and his lively self reappeared. Humming a little tune, he set to work in the kitchen. Tsuru felt like humming, too. Toshio brought her a gin and ginger ale with a slice of lemon; for himself he'd poured a neat whisky with plenty of ice. After the first sip he said feelingly, "Ah, that's a good whisky. Yes indeed." At that moment he seemed rapt in the taste. Tsuyama would sip this same whisky pensively, his thoughts elsewhere, but even when he noticed its quality he wasn't likely to exclaim aloud about it, Tsuru thought.

Toshio suggested they put on a record. After he'd deliberated over the choice—judging this one too gloomy and that too noisy—the jazz violin of Stefan Grappeli, elegant and a little rough, began to play. They exchanged a comment or two and then fell silent. Seemingly engrossed in the music, they raised their glasses to their lips by turns. When the ice was uncovered, Toshio poured himself another whisky.

"I think it's a great goal." He had not been following the music, then.

"Goal? Whose?"

Toshio indicated Tsuru with a motion of his head. "A specialty of your own. Your pottery."

Once again, Tsuru noted, he'd deftly avoided addressing her by name. Toshio had never called her "Tsuru," nor did he call her

"Mrs. Tsuyama," of course, nor any of the familiar forms of "you." Tsuru had watched his struggles with some amusement as he shunned any form of address.

"Oh, it's nowhere near being a specialty yet."

"But it's an admirable goal."

Quickly taking her almost empty glass, Toshio went into the kitchen. She had been going to decline but couldn't get the words out.

"What am I going to do? I hate to think," Toshio called from the kitchen. Tsuru laughed quietly as the gin and the playful violin began to set her at ease with the world.

"I don't know a whole lot about myself or life," he went on. "All I know is what I like. That's as clear as can be. It's so clear it makes life difficult. But I can't change the fact that I know what I like."

Tsuru chuckled again.

She wasn't sure how much he had to drink after that. Certainly he had been drunk, but he hadn't forgotten his manners. Instead, the puzzling reserve gradually vanished and the mood that the whisky encouraged led to a conversation that might have taken place at the back of a classroom, about themselves and their limited experience of love.

Tsuru was enjoying herself too much to turn down a third drink. But she felt drowsiness tugging at her and took small, cautious sips of the strong liquid.

The record that was on at that moment—there'd been several, she'd lost count—was an organ fugue that reverberated deep down inside her. Toshio was describing the poetry reading he'd gone to that evening. He'd been invited by a monthly magazine to which he'd sent several pieces of his own. He confessed his longing to write poetry and added, "But I don't get on with poets. I'm not a bit like them. They don't ever seem to get their teeth into anything in life.

"I wish you could have seen me read, though," he said. "There were thirty people in the audience, you know. I should've told you and Sensei about it, Tsu. You're the people I wanted most to hear me.''

Toshio had used her nickname for the first time. It hung for an instant in the air and was gone as casually as if he'd been using it all along.

"I'd like you to hear me, Tsu.''

"Read me one now," Tsuru said, fighting off sleep.

"Okay, here goes.''

Toshio lurched to his feet, straightened his rumpled clothes, and announced grandly, "Allow me to present the distinguished poet Toshio Kotani, who will read one of his undiscovered works of genius.''

Tsuru lost the fight against her sleepiness. She had no idea whether Toshio read his poetry or not. She awoke to a touch on her lips. From her lips it moved to her eyelids, cheeks, hair, and to her lips again. It felt like a fingertip. It was a pleasurable touch, and Tsuru kept her eyes closed.

Toshio's voice murmured hoarsely, "I love you. I can't help myself.'' She didn't hesitate to return his kiss and the pressure of his body, his words reechoing inside her.

Tsuru could only think she must have loved Toshio before that night; she suspected also that if it hadn't been for that night she might have contentedly gone without ever speaking of love to him.

She pushed this suspicion to the back of her mind. It might be so; but there was nothing she could do now.

7

"What's going on? I got such a shock when I heard.'' Tsuru had barely opened the front door before Kanako was searching her face.

She hid her alarm. "What?'' She followed Kanako, who hadn't answered but stepped inside with a preoccupied air. "What do you mean?'' Kanako sat down at the dining table and, brushing back her dyed brown hair with one hand, stared intently at Tsuru again.

Tsuru lowered herself to a chair but couldn't remain there. She was almost on her feet again, offering a cup of coffee, when Kanako laid a hand over hers on the table and said quickly, "No, I can't stay." Reluctantly, she sat down.

"I know. About you and Kotani."

"Oh, that."

Even as she spoke offhandedly, praying she could carry it off, Tsuru felt a blush flaring around her ears. She was on the spot and would have to say something. What slipped out was a question: "Who did you hear it from?"

"Kotani."

"Ah."

Nodding casually, Tsuru was secretly stunned.

Since his first phone call five days before, she'd been in the habit of dialing Toshio's number the moment Tsuyama went out. She'd already done so this very morning. Yet Toshio had chatted about the usual inconsequential things.

After sighing heavily, Kanako provided a clue to the puzzle. "I thought it was odd that you two hadn't been round to The Gendarme lately. I guessed something was up, and so I asked him over just now and got it out of him."

They'd talked on the phone from some time after ten o'clock till nearly eleven. Kanako must have called Toshio after that. The unseen events began to take shape in Tsuru's mind and she relaxed very slightly.

"I said to him, 'There's something going on, isn't there?' and he blabbed the whole story."

There was more to this bluntness of Kanako's than her knowing Toshio well. Tsuru laughed faintly, intimidated by her manner, and said, "He likes to talk."

"He certainly does. Chatting away about a thing like that! He talked his head off about how he loves you." The tone was accusing, and Tsuru felt sure it was she who stood accused.

Toshio had said in one of their secret calls, "I'm bursting to tell people about you. I want to boast to everyone I see. I want to take you everywhere and show you off. It's agony having to wait."

This passionate declaration now came back to her in a different light—as a warning of his impulsiveness.

How could he, Tsuru thought angrily—how could he have confessed at the first hint that somebody was curious? Her shame before Kanako was acute.

"Why didn't you tell me?" said Kanako gently.

There was no adequate reason. Tsuru mumbled, "I didn't mean to hide it, but before I had a chance to tell you the situation got complicated. . . ."

"So I heard. Three months, wasn't it?"

What *had* Toshio said? What? How? How much? The need to find out wasn't as strong as her terror of facing Kanako like this.

Kanako regarded her as she might a friend who had contracted an incurable disease. Her eyes were filled with the desire to save her. Under that unbearable gaze Tsuru felt like an insect with its legs plucked off.

"Must you?" Kanako asked. Since Tsuru failed to take her meaning, she went on, "What about poor Tsuyama? After he's been so good to you."

Tsuru shook her head, both in answer and because she didn't want to hear any more. "It's too late. There's nothing anyone can do."

"Won't you think it over? Seriously. I wouldn't say this if he were just any husband, you know. A man like Tsuyama is hard to find. How can you think of leaving him for Kotani? There must be something wrong with you."

In her heart, which she had quickly closed against Kanako's words, Tsuru thought that perhaps she might be a little crazed at present.

"Kotani is wrong for you, I'm absolutely certain of it. You're making a mistake. I don't want to see you unhappy." Coming from a very dear friend, this advice was especially unwelcome.

"What makes you so sure I'll be unhappy?"

Unprepared for the question, Kanako groped for an answer, lowering her eyes to Tsuru's clasped fingers on the tabletop. "Of course Kotani isn't a bad person. He'd make a good friend. But as a partner for you, he's unsuitable."

The word struck Tsuru with the strangeness of some new piece of slang. She had never considered Toshio's suitability.

"It's not as if we're getting married."

"Living together's the same thing."

"We're not going to live together."

Kanako gave her a quizzical look, just as Tsuyama had. "But Kotani thinks you will."

"I guess so."

Tsuru's heart sank at the prospect of eventually having to explain herself to him. She was even less inclined to account for the discrepancy to Kanako. When it became obvious that Tsuru was not going to say more, Kanako broke the silence again.

"I don't approve of him." She said this slowly and with feeling. "I asked if he thought he could support you. He said no. That would have been bad enough, but he assured me you could earn a living with your pottery."

Tsuru could picture Toshio saying this. It was very much in character. She smiled.

"I'd have thought," Kanako complained, "that he'd at least claim he was going to. If he cared."

Tsuru wanted her friend to understand that Toshio did care. But how could she make her see? Nonplussed, Tsuru dug hard at one thumbnail with the other.

"So then I asked him if he could guarantee you'd be happy with him, and he said no one can guarantee another person's happiness! He strikes me as totally insincere."

Tsuru dug more furiously at her nail. She thought of Toshio answering Kanako's questions with the same unguarded sincerity that he showed her. His answers were totally honest. Of course no one could guarantee another's happiness.

"That's all very well in theory, I suppose. . . ." Kanako was still not satisfied. "But then—"

Unable to cry "Enough!" Tsuru merely put her head on one side.

"I told him, 'Tsuru is more stubborn than she looks, and a bit childish with it. She's not an easy woman to deal with. Think you'll get on?' And you know what he said? 'I give it two years.' Well!"

A gust of cold air swept through Tsuru. The figure of Toshio, always clear in her mind's eye, began to blur and change shape eerily, like the moon on a rippling water surface.

She couldn't imagine so cold an answer from the Toshio she knew. Had he said that? Why would Kanako lie? Suppose he had— was that what he thought? Could he have made such a cool estimation of their love?

Tsuru's mind raced, attempting to put the eerily rippling shape back the way it had been.

It might have been a joke. Knowing Toshio, he was probably being flippant to head off Kanako's persistent questioning. At this thought the swaying figure steadied a little.

Tsuru badly wanted to know whether Toshio had looked serious when he'd given that answer, whether he'd laughed or appeared not to care what he said. But she couldn't bring herself to ask and make her condition seem more hopeless than ever. And anyway Kanako couldn't have told her what Toshio meant. Inwardly Tsuru was crying out for him. She looked closely at Kanako.

Kanako's face had lost its earlier assurance. Tsuru felt a liking for her, and let out a small self-conscious laugh.

"This is no laughing matter," said Kanako, but she, too, was smiling.

"I'm sorry if I've upset you."

"Oh, never mind about me."

Tsuru appealed to her friend, and to herself as well: "Perhaps I will be unhappy, as you say. But I've made my choice and I can only go through with it. It's my life. Let me do it my way, will you, please?"

Kanako grinned. "I envy you."

"What for?"

"Being able to lose your head over a man."

"I must look a fool."

"Well, yes, there is a sort of half-crazed gleam in your eyes. All the same . . ." Kanako added, straight-faced now, "you're looking very good, you know."

"Thanks."

After pausing to see Tsuru smile happily, she went on, "But whatever happens you won't do anything to hurt Tsuyama, will you? If you've sworn to stay away from Toshio for three months, keep your word. You will, won't you?"

Of course she would, she protested guiltily.

Kanako had been gone only a few moments when Tsuyama came home.

"Oh, you didn't run into Kanako?" Tsuru asked.

"No, was she here? Did she want something?"

"She just dropped in for a chat," Tsuru answered.

8

Kanako had made up her mind that Toshio was unreliable, insincere, a good-for-nothing. Tsuru was resigned to the fact that certain things about him might strike an onlooker that way. She couldn't hold it against Kanako.

What did make her uncomfortable was the surprising ease with which her own faith in Toshio had been shaken by Kanako's words. She knew Toshio. She knew him through the evidence of her own eyes, ears, and hands. That was the real Toshio, and the picture that Kanako's words had sketched in the air was an illusion. Yet while she had looked on blankly, the illusion had swayed her own image of Toshio.

Once disturbed, the figure was distressingly slow to return to its original clear contours.

She longed to hear Toshio's voice. If only she could talk to him, everything would surely fall into place and the feeling of sadness would go away.

She counted the rings of the phone by the stairs in his distant apartment. On the sixth the ringing broke off and Toshio panted, "Hello? Hello?"

As the first ring reached his ears, which seemed to exist to listen for this sound, Toshio would always hurl himself at the phone, rocking the whole building. She could just see it. This was reassuring already: Toshio was Toshio, as she'd known all along.

"Toshi, you've been talking to Kanako, haven't you?" She'd barely finished before he burst out:

"Right. I was at my wits' end." He did sound harassed. "How did you know? It was only yesterday."

"She came over here afterward."

"Oh?" He didn't ask why. He seemed uninterested in anything that Kanako might have had to say. "It was the last thing I expected," he went on.

"Me, too. When I'd asked you especially not to talk to anybody."

After Kanako's visit Tsuru had decided to make it perfectly clear that his easygoing ways had to stop.

"I'm sorry." He apologized so readily, Tsuru lost the chance to drive her point home. "It was a mistake. I should never have gone along so unsuspectingly. She said she had something to tell me that concerned you but she couldn't talk over the phone. It bothered me so much I just had to go. It was careless of me and I'm sorry."

Her annoyance was fading. In Toshio's position she'd have done the same.

"I guess it wasn't your fault. But did you have to tell her everything when all she said was 'there's something going on'?"

"I know, I know. I should've put on an act. But I'm hopeless at that sort of thing. And I don't want to hide, anyway, I'd rather have it out in the open. Besides, she is a good friend of yours, and I'm fond of her myself. I guess she caught me off guard."

Unable to blame him any further, Tsuru heaved a sigh. At least she'd gotten it off her chest.

"It was amazingly sharp of her, though, wasn't it? When she suddenly suggested there was something between us I nearly fell off my chair," Toshio said, sounding agitated still. It was amazing, Tsuru thought, belatedly.

"Toshi, you hadn't been dropping hints, had you?"

"Of course not," he insisted. "She came straight out with the question almost the moment I got there. Even then I bluffed it out for a while, but she was determined. 'It's no good trying to cover up, I know all about it.' That was what she said. And in the end I broke down."

Kanako had spoken of a very casual confession. Probably both versions were true from the speaker's point of view. The conversation they'd had was lost forever; there was no way of knowing the facts.

As these thoughts ran through her head, she was prompting him to go on. What had been neatly contained between her lover and herself had overflowed its bounds; it was becoming hard to grasp the whole. Tsuru felt everything slipping away.

"Of course *you* haven't been talking to her, have you, Tsu?"

"No. Remember when we called in at The Gendarme together, around the beginning of February, on our way home from the poster exhibition?"

"Ah, yes. The day we ran into my friend."

"I hadn't seen her since then. That's what she thought was so odd, in fact—that we hadn't been in."

"Could she have caught on back then?"

"Hmm."

"We both tend to show how we feel. Maybe she could tell."

"Well, I don't know about you, but I don't think I've been so open with Kanako." Tsuru couldn't be certain, nevertheless. Kanako had read her mind often enough in the past.

"Oh no!" Toshio gave a wild cry. "Could Kanako have fallen for me?"

Startled, Tsuru said, "What makes you think that?"

"Well, they say that when you're in love you have a sixth sense about such things, don't they?" He managed to sound quite intrigued by the idea. Tsuru's astonishment turned to indignation.

"I'm afraid she's too choosy. She likes her men handsome."

"Oh. Pity."

There was one other thing Tsuru had to check before the matter could be passed off with a joke.

"The other day, I ran into your friend outside the apartment."

"So he said."

"He gave me the impression that he knew. About us."

"Ah. Now him, I did tell."

He said this so lightly that Tsuru shrieked, "Not him, too!" In place of Toshio she shook the hairbrush she'd been toying with on her knee.

"Well, you know . . ." As if to escape the shaking, he pleaded, "I'd already told him when you swore me to silence. By that time I couldn't help it, could I?"

Tsuru let out a groan.

"And, besides, what's wrong with wanting someone to know about us? It's different for you, you've got your marriage. But suppose—just suppose you died tomorrow, okay? I'd be the only one who'd ever have known what we had. I couldn't bear being left with nothing but my own memories. When I'm not even allowed to see your face, I sometimes wonder whether it isn't all in my mind—your existence, our being in love. As long as I can talk to someone I can convince myself it's real. Otherwise, believe me, I couldn't stand this."

So Toshio, too, had to live with an image that was easily swayed. Tsuru hung her head. When he broke off, she said only, "I know." There was a pause as if to let her quiet words sink in, then Toshio said, "Yes." She became aware of the receiver clutched in her hand, and once she noticed its clumsiness she couldn't rid herself of the sensation. Toshio ended the silence.

"We can trust him. It'll be okay."

"He's at your university, isn't he?"

"Yes, but not in Sensei's course. He'll never meet him. And, unlike me, he's the soul of discretion."

Tsuru couldn't help asking, though cautiously, "Have you warned him?"

"Yeah. If he talks he forfeits his precious kerosene heater and his leather jacket."

"He'd better not."

"Well, the leather jacket I can do without, but the heater's a very attractive proposition. It's good as new. If he's going to forfeit it, I hope he'll do it while the weather's still cold."

"Toshi!"

"Sorry. Look, don't be so nervous. Trust me, it'll be all right. Kanako's the real danger—she knows Sensei and your other friends, doesn't she?"

"I trust Kanako absolutely. She'd never make trouble for me."

"Then there's no problem."

"You haven't spoken to anyone else, and . . ."

She had meant it to come out casually, but Toshio wasn't fooled. "Hey," he said, "I've had about as much as I can take of this checking up."

Reflecting later on their conversation as she got ready to go out, Tsuru realized that in the end she had failed to ask the one question that mattered to her most: had he been serious when he'd given their relationship two years?

Now that she was intensely aware of his presence it seemed

foolish to have minded such a little thing. It had surely been a joke. If only Toshio were so detached she'd have nothing to worry about. The thought buoyed up her spirits.

9

Leaning over Tsuru's shoulder and watching her hard at work kneading clay, Kimi Kuramoto said, "Mrs. Tsuyama, when you have a moment, please . . . ," then withdrew into the small office that opened off the studio.

Tsuru left her work and followed, wiping her hands on a towel she carried around her neck. Kimi motioned her to a chair and carefully closed the door; then, seating herself correctly across from Tsuru, she closed her eyes for several moments.

Kimi Kuramoto's husband was a professor at the university. Tsuyama looked up to the older man as a trusted expert in their field, and Kuramoto had extended his help whenever it was needed. When Tsuyama had introduced his wife to the studio, the same relationship had established itself: Tsuru admired Kimi, and Kimi took Tsuru under her wing.

Tsuru could not, however, confide in Kimi. She was somewhat in awe of this woman five or six years older than Tsuyama who seldom lost her self-assurance.

Facing her in this room whose door was rarely closed, watching her choose her words so deliberately, Tsuru was more awed than usual. She braced herself for whatever might be coming. Kimi's eyes calmly opened and rested on her.

"Mrs. Tsuyama, I've heard a most unfortunate rumor concerning you."

Tsuru was forced to ask "What rumor is that?" Her voice sounded false even to herself, as if she were reciting a line from a play.

"The rumor is that you and your husband aren't getting on."
Kimi broke off again; this time no lines came to Tsuru's mind.
"And, furthermore, that you are having an affair."

The words descended on her like a screeching horde of monkeys
that flung her, a naked adulteress, on the ground before Kimi. Tsuru
turned pale and lowered her eyes. The attack had left her without
the strength of mind to pick herself up and cover her nakedness.

"Not a very nice rumor, is it?" Kimi's expression softened. "But
then rumors never are. I have no intention of asking you whether
it's true. I know very well how good your husband is to you and
how much you appreciate him, and I know that you're both sensible
people. Personally I think the rumor is laughable. Such an ideal
marriage, the envy of us all—why, it's preposterous."

Before she could stop herself Tsuru had let out a pained laugh. It
was the only answer she could give. But it meant she'd inadvertently agreed.

"All the same, there's no smoke without fire, as they say. Oh, I
don't mean to suggest that the rumor has any substance. I'm quite
confident it has none. The fact that people are talking in this way,
though, does perhaps indicate a need for you to think twice about
your own behavior."

Tsuru nodded meekly. Kimi had spared her the necessity of an
outright denial, yet now she wished she'd lied, or even confessed.
As it was she couldn't find out how far the rumor went—nor just
how far Kimi believed it.

Tsuru wondered forlornly how much longer the probing would go
on; there was not a thing she could do, however.

"What are your views on marriage, my dear?"

Tsuru gave Kimi a polite but puzzled look.

"As you know," the older woman explained, "what with wom-
en's lib and so forth, there's a growing tendency these days to blame
marriage for depriving women of independence, freedom, a career."

Tsuru thought a little and answered honestly, "That's not what I think."

"Neither do I," said Kimi. "I've never neglected my home for my work. I've brought up three children, and although I must say my husband takes more looking after than Mr. Tsuyama, I've always managed to keep a balance between work and the home. I've never thought of marriage as holding me back. And I expect I'm more independent-minded than most."

These were the very qualities that Tsuru had always admired.

"I'm afraid," Kimi continued, "that the women who argue that way must be quite lazy and selfish." Her left eyebrow lifted sharply, then returned to its mild curve.

"In any case, if one chooses to marry one mustn't make life unpleasant for one's husband and children. That's the least one can do. It's not easy when one is working, but it was my own selfish decision and I mustn't complain. I'd rather give up my work than make my family suffer. After all, which is more important? I love my pottery and hope to work at it as long as I live. But it's nothing compared to my home. I have my work only because I have my home. I can enjoy my work only because I have my husband and children. Knowing this has kept me going."

Kimi paused. She must have worked very hard indeed, thought Tsuru with an oppressive sense of being too lax with herself.

"Lately you've been very dedicated. You're establishing your name as a potter, and with a little more effort I expect you could make a career. I'm delighted for you, of course, but I would hate to see you neglect your home on that account."

It wasn't excessive enthusiasm for her work that had made her want to leave Tsuyama or brought her together with Toshio. If there was any connection, it was the prospect of supporting herself. With the resolve to go it alone had come a renewed enthusiasm for the work itself.

"If you're going to act selfishly and neglect Mr. Tsuyama, I think it'd be better if you gave up pottery."

Tsuru was studying her hands. They were flecked with dried clay.

"Mr. Tsuyama is a fine man. If you don't take proper care of him, you'll deserve what you get." Kimi was smiling.

Her eyes still downcast, Tsuru answered, "Yes."

"Now, back to work! I'm so sorry to have interrupted you."

"Oh, no, I'm sorry if I've caused you to worry."

As she followed Kimi in getting to her feet, Tsuru found the nerve to say "Do you mind if I ask where you heard the rumor?"

Kimi stared at her for a while, then said, "I don't think I should tell you that."

"But . . ."

The word burst out with an urgency she couldn't disguise. Kimi asked, her head a little on one side, "Does it bother you?" Then she turned her eyes away and said, "The world's a smaller place than you might suppose, especially at the university. The students talk, and you can't hope to keep a secret for long. And besides . . ." She placed her hand on Tsuru's shoulder. "Remember that men are proud of their conquests. They like to kiss and tell."

As she finished speaking, the hand resting on Tsuru's shoulder gave her a push toward the studio.

10

Tsuru could clearly picture a gigantic spindle-shaped eye hovering amid the spring haze. It glided soundlessly overhead, soaring into the sky or swooping down over the city to keep her under constant observation. She couldn't tell whether the impassive eye was that of a demon or a god, but after Kanako's visit and Kimi's warning she began to believe in its existence.

Having shed her mask of decency, Tsuru had at first thought of herself as boldly taking a risk. When she'd set out on her course of deception, her guilt had overflowed as tenderness toward her husband, a genuine concern that led her to care for him better than

ever. With the discovery that she could devote herself to her husband after an intimate conversation with Toshio she had even told
herself that lying was easier than she'd thought.

Now, however, Tsuru was cowering beneath an unseen gaze that
seemed to come from nowhere. It was a dark reminder of her child-
hood fears when she'd been told God would know that she'd been bad.

Summoning her failing courage, Tsuru tried to catch a glimpse of
whatever it was that revealed itself only by its huge eye.

How could they have given themselves away? What had they
done, where had they been? Tsuru went back over everything she
and Toshio had done since they'd fallen in love. They hadn't met
secretly. They had certainly gone out without Tsuyama, but always
to exhibitions or films. It would have taken a particularly suspicious
mind to discern anything but friendship in their closeness.

A complete stranger might perhaps have taken them for lovers,
but anyone who knew Tsuru and Toshio and Tsuyama would see
nothing untoward in their being together.

There was one scene that chilled her to recall: under the darkened
movie theater's armrest their fingers had intertwined as the screen's
blue light played over them. That would have been sufficient. But
who could have seen them and where had that person been among
all those unfamiliar faces in the darkness? Though convinced they
couldn't possibly have been seen, Tsuru was a little sorry that she'd
responded when Toshio's hand had reached for hers.

That time when she'd gone to Toshio's apartment worried her,
too. She had met no one but his roommate, yet she couldn't be
certain that her presence had escaped notice.

Inevitably her thoughts were drawn to the mysterious eye. She
tried to shrug off the sinister gaze, persuading herself that her fears
of someone, somewhere, were merely childish fancies. "Somewhere"
would turn out to exist, and "someone" to have a human face.

Kanako's face had made its appearance some five days after her
first talk with Toshio on the phone; Kimi's, about six days later. By

the time these two had entered into the mystery, her affair with Toshio was already confined to the phone. Their timing might have nothing to do with the supernatural but it was eerie enough.

Kanako had said she guessed, which Toshio had called amazingly sharp. Tsuru had also found her friend's intuition amazing but not impossible, since Kanako was the person who had most often witnessed them together and—as she'd pointed out—their sudden avoidance of The Gendarme had provided another clue. She probably had been guessing, for if there'd been any more to it Kanako was the kind of friend who'd warn Tsuru to be more careful.

It was Kimi that she couldn't understand. She wouldn't reveal her source, knowing surely that she must be plunging Tsuru into anxious misery. Had she meant to administer strong medicine to a loose woman?

Her parting remarks, while perhaps offering a clue to the puzzle, had only worsened Tsuru's anxiety and bewilderment. "The world's a smaller place than you might suppose, especially at the university. The students talk, and you can't hope to keep a secret for long." Tsuru knew of no one—apart from Kanako and Toshio's friend— who could have been gossiping. She didn't believe it was Kanako. The world might be small, but the connection between Kanako and Kimi was too remote altogether, unless she herself supplied it. Then was it Toshio's friend after all? "The students talk." Had Toshio's friend started a rumor that had reached Professor Kuramoto? When she thought of Tsuyama on the same campus, Tsuru felt she had one foot on each side of a crevice opening in the earth.

Toshio had insisted on his friend's reliability. If she accepted her own trust in Kanako she had to accept his trust in his friend. But mingled with her anxiety and confusion was a creeping fog of distrust toward Toshio himself.

"Remember that men are proud of their conquests. They like to kiss and tell." Kimi could only have had one man in mind.

A vision of Toshio sneering "I give it two years" bore down on

Tsuru with a new reality. At the thought of how she might appear to him—a hysterical older woman clutching desperately at a casual affair—the shame almost drove her to smash her world and the people in it. She still couldn't imagine Toshio—the Toshio she knew—boasting of her as a conquest. She could, however, imagine any number of scenes in which the story slipped out by accident. It had been Toshio, not Tsuru, who had confided in both Kanako and his friend.

"I said to him, 'There's something going on, isn't there?' and he blabbed the whole story," Kanako had told her.

"When I'm not even allowed to see your face, I sometimes wonder whether it isn't all in my mind—your existence, our being in love. As long as I can talk to someone I can convince myself it's real." There was no guarantee that he wouldn't be asked again what was going on, or suddenly seek reassurance from another friend.

Even so, she couldn't blame Toshio. He had been willing to confront Tsuyama; he hadn't been afraid of being the guilty party who hurt her husband. It was Tsuru who was afraid. It was she who was dishonest, nursing her fear while pursuing her love affair as recklessly as ever.

Saving face was a duty she had imposed on herself, and Toshio had never been under any obligation to share it. She reminded herself of this as the burden grew monstrously heavy. It was Tsuru alone, and not Toshio, who was exposed to the gaze of the immense eye.

"I don't get it. If a rumor like that had been going around I'd have heard it. But I haven't heard a thing," said Toshio the next day on the phone. Tsuru had brought him up-to-date, omitting only Kimi's final words.

"But the target of the gossip is often the last to know. It's already got as far as Professor Kuramoto's wife."

"Damn. What the hell is going on?" said Toshio fiercely. "I'll check again, but I don't think my roommate can have started it—he's never let me down before. And he's the only one who knows. So there's no way it could have gotten around at the university." His unaccustomed seriousness made Tsuru start to think she'd been wrong to suspect Toshio. She would have liked to believe in him wholly and let him carry half the burden.

"What about Sensei?"

"He doesn't seem to have heard a thing, thank goodness."

"He hasn't changed at all?"

"No. He acts as though nothing's happened. Last night, he—" She caught her breath sharply; she had said too much. She could hardly tell Toshio that she'd sensed no change in Tsuyama even when he made love to her the previous night. She sidestepped just in time. "He was the same as ever."

"If he'd heard anything he'd bring it up, wouldn't he?" Toshio was untroubled.

"I think so."

"Whew."

So Toshio did care about her promise, thought Tsuru, rejoicing.

"Let's get this straight, okay? I haven't said a word. I'd like to shout it from the rooftops but I've stopped myself."

"Keep it up."

"Well, now and then I do mention that I'm in love. That's not counted, is it? As long as nobody knows who with."

Tsuru was alarmed again, afraid that people might guess, but she refrained from saying so. She was worn out.

"Maybe we should give up these phone calls?" she said quietly. If only they abided by the ban she wouldn't have so much to fear. Perhaps, too, these meager contacts were driving Toshio to talk. At the very least, if she stopped phoning she could prevent his leaking that particular secret. For how could she face her husband if, instead of a mere rumor of the affair, he were to learn of these telephone trysts?

"Hey!" Toshio was shocked. "No way!" He spelled it out carefully: "Listen, you and I are the only ones who know about these calls. Just us. I haven't told Kanako and I haven't told my friend. It's our secret. No one but God will ever know."

"To tell you the truth, it's God I'm worried about."

"Now don't get panicky. That's absurd and you know it. In any case, Tsu, suppose the story does get out. What would it matter in the end? Even if Sensei beat me up I wouldn't let you go."

Most likely she would call again the next day, thought Tsuru.

11

Tsuru was watching Tsuyama across the table as he neatly slit three sides of a paper sachet of stomach medicine, gathered the powder in the middle, and poured it into his wide-open mouth. His face took on a pathetic look as he did so.

It was a routine of his—one that had been occurring more frequently of late. Undoubtedly Tsuru's affair was to blame. He may have been carrying on as though nothing had happened, but he was suffering all the same, and the thought filled Tsuru with self-reproach. His complexion, never very healthy at the best of times, was duller than ever.

Several times she had urged him nervously to see a doctor, but Tsuyama only gave vague replies and gulped down stomach medicine.

As she rested her chin on her hand and watched his Adam's apple (which was smaller than Toshio's) move in his stretched throat, she predicted that her husband would come to her bed again that night. The rate at which he took medicine was not the only thing that had increased recently.

Sex had once been so small a part of their marriage that Tsuru had almost forgotten that the union of husband and wife was sexual. She had even had the idea that, while not lacking in sensuality, she was indifferent to sex. She had had to revise that opinion of herself when she'd become involved with Toshio: at least she was not as indifferent as she'd thought. She felt an uninhibited sexuality very like Toshio's make its presence happily known inside her.

But only with Toshio. With her husband, as always, Tsuru was close to forgetting the sexual side of their relations.

For some reason, though, when he began to want her more often after she'd spoken of leaving him, sex with her husband loomed large, a sheer rocklike obstacle.

The familiar act itself was never difficult; the difficulty was with her own emotions—less the sense of letting Toshio down than the terrible awkwardness she felt with her husband. She genuinely wanted to satisfy Tsuyama's wishes whatever they might be. Yet if this meant welcoming him into her bed, she became a fraud who would calmly make love with one man while her mind was on another. If she rejected Tsuyama she became a cruel tormentor who turned the knife in his wound.

Either way, in Tsuyama's arms Tsuru could only be in the wrong. When she asked herself how he must see her, she had an unnerving vision of herself as his prisoner being paraded naked through the streets. She could see no other way out, though, and would attempt with her eyes closed to cross the torrent of conflicts. The three-month time limit was her only hope.

Tsuyama may or may not have known her thoughts, but when he had swallowed the medicine with a grimace and taken a sip of water he suddenly caught Tsuru's eye and smiled. She returned the smile easily and said, as she had said a number of times already, "You really should see a doctor."

"One of these days," Tsuyama answered as he had already done a number of times. Then he added, his expression clouding, "I doubt that it would do any good. Stomach troubles are often psychological." Anxiety grated inside her. Tsuyama looked searchingly at her. Her breathing was shallow and her heart beat oppressively.

"You're not seeing Toshio at present, are you?"

The blood drained from her face.

"No."

"I thought not. Of course you're not." Tsuyama tilted his head to one side. Forcing herself to steady her gaze, she said, "Why do you ask?"

"I'm sorry. Actually, I'd heard something odd." Drawing the glass of water toward him, he stared into it without drinking. "A certain person warned me. It seems there's a rumor going around. The story is that you're still seeing him. I knew it couldn't be true."

"That's awful." She smiled, her lips twitching at the corners. "Why would anyone say that? That I'm *still* seeing him?"

"It wasn't very pleasant to have to listen to, and I didn't ask for details, but they claimed to have seen you together, or heard you together, quite recently."

"That's impossible." Tsuru seized a cloth and rubbed the table-top. After watching her for a moment, Tsuyama said, "I must have gotten that part wrong, then. All the same, it was something of a shock to be told of a rumor like that."

"I'm sorry." Without thinking, Tsuru bowed her head.

"You needn't apologize. I trust you are keeping your promise? You haven't talked to anybody, have you?"

Tsuru could only nod wordlessly.

"Then I wonder how the rumor could have gotten started?"

"I wonder."

Tsuru knew of just one possible source if the rumor referred to the present. This was the fifth day since she'd hesitated over whether to end the phone calls. She regretted her decision now.

"Oh well," Tsuyama said as he got to his feet, "you can't stop people talking. It's rather unfortunate, but I'm glad to know you haven't broken your promise. It can't have been easy for you."

Coming around the table, he slipped his arms about her from behind as she started to rise and pressed his face into the back of her neck. Tsuru closed her eyes resignedly.

12

"Toshi, I want to do it this way. I mean it."

"Hang on, Tsu. I've checked and he swears he hasn't breathed a word. And he says he hasn't heard any rumors on campus."

"But Sensei did."

"Who on earth from?"

"I don't know!"

"Tsu."

"And what's more, he's heard we're still seeing each other. All I can think is that someone has found out about these calls."

"How could anyone find out? That's stupid. It's impossible."

"Then how did Professor Kuramoto's wife know? How does Sensei know?"

"Calm down, Tsu. It's weird, I know. It's bizarre. There's something behind all this. That's what I think. If we're ever going to find out what it is, we have to keep in touch."

"I don't want to. I can't stand this any more. It's much simpler to stop calling. If we aren't in touch then we needn't worry, whatever rumors are being spread about us. Don't you see, Toshi?"

"No, I don't. I can't agree to that."

"There's only a little over two months to go."

"No. Who knows what will happen in the meantime? By then you might not want to leave him."

"Why won't you trust me?"

"I trust you now. But listen, Tsu, people's feelings change. They change in ways we can't control."

"Yours, too?"

"I guess so. If we lost touch there's no telling what might happen."

"I see. So that's all it means to you?"

"Don't get me wrong, Tsu. I don't want to let anything change my love for you. Or yours for me. That's what I'm saying."

"I won't change, you'll see. No matter how long we're apart."

"Well, I'd say the same about me, but—"

"Then no more phone calls, all right?"

"Tsu, are you leaving me?"

"Did I say that?"

"It comes to the same thing. I'll die."

"Don't be silly, Toshi. Please try and understand. At the end of May I'll come flying to you. I'll keep a diary every day instead of talking to you and I'll give it to you afterward to read. How's that? I'm not going to phone till then."

"I don't like this at all."

"I've made up my mind. Good-bye, Toshi. Till the end of May."

"No! No!"

Tearing the receiver from her ear as it continued to howl "No!" She jammed it down hard. Her pent-up tears overflowed and dripped onto her hands pressed tightly over the phone as if to prevent Toshio's voice from leaking out. Immediately the phone bell rang under her hands. She pressed down harder. The ringing went on and on, only to fall silent at last with a forlorn tinkle.

That night Tsuru had a disturbing dream.

She was dozing at the foot of a great tree covered in the fresh green leaves of early summer. From time to time a cool breeze rustled the leaves overhead. After a while she became aware of being softly held against someone's chest. She wanted to ask "Who's there?" but she was too sleepy. The chest and the arms had a very familiar feel.

Ah, she thought, it's Toshi. Of course, it's June already, that explains why I'm with Toshi. It was a good feeling. The hands stroked her back, her cheeks, her throat. Steadily they began to tighten, choking her. When she forced her reluctant lids open, for an instant she saw Toshio's face wearing a fiendish grin. But the sunlight, dazzling through the leaves, prevented her getting a better look.

She was being choked harder and harder. Unable to move or scream, she made a desperate effort to see who it was. A pair of silver scissors flashed before her eyes. It could have been Tsuyama. It could have been Toshio. In the same moment as the horrible realization came to her that it was neither, but a grotesque demon, she woke. Just before she did she heard her own voice moaning.

It was early the following evening that Toshio appeared on Tsuyama's front doorstep.

Tsuru was at the kitchen sink when he arrived. Tsuyama, who was reading in the living room, answered the bell. As he was gone a long time Tsuru turned off the gushing faucet and listened: she heard a voice she couldn't believe she was hearing. With dripping hands she moved toward the closed door that led into the hall passage. The voice was unmistakably Toshio's. "Never mind that," she heard, "please let me see her."

Tsuru quietly pushed the door open and stepped into the passage. She hadn't considered what she would do when she reached the hallway; she just let her feet take her there. Toshio was watching her over Tsuyama's shoulder, his face white and drained. Under his fierce brows, his eyes gleamed with a grim intensity that could have struck Tsuru down.

She felt her own eyes return their fire as she prepared to defend herself. Yet she had never wanted so much to hold him. She stood firmly behind Tsuyama, who slowly drew aside and saw her.

Toshio's faltering gaze shifted to Tsuyama. "Sensei, please. Let us be together. I'll take any punishment. Please."

Toshio bowed his head deeply. Tsuyama said quietly, not taking his eyes off Tsuru's profile, "I'm not the one to ask. It's Tsuru's problem. It's for Tsuru to decide."

Toshio looked around at Tsuru. "Tsu. Let's go."

As she remained silent, the fierceness of his gaze was dulled by a flicker of uncertainty.

"Tsu. Come just as you are. Let's go."

If they had been alone Tsuru might have hugged Toshio's hot body with all her strength. But in front of Tsuyama this love could not continue to be.

"Why did you come?" she said in a low, hard mutter. Toshio's hand came to rest on the thigh of her jeans, where it moved up and down.

"I've had enough of this." As if to make up for the weak voice in which he had begun, he shouted now, "I thought we loved each other."

Out of the corner of her eye Tsuru could see Tsuyama with his arms folded.

"So?" her calm voice replied.

"So we have to live that way. Together."

The terror of losing Toshio was sounding a frantic alarm at the back of Tsuru's mind. But their exchange was gaining momentum and couldn't be stopped.

"Don't be too sure. Even if I left Sensei I'm not planning to live with you, Toshi."

Toshio's drawn lips turned apple green. Tsuru was fascinated by their color. Quivering, the pale lips forced out the words "Then you *are* leaving me."

The moment he finished speaking, his large palm struck Tsuru's cheek. As she reeled back against Tsuyama, her husband caught her firmly and shouted loud enough to rattle the walls, "Get your hands off her!" As Tsuru regained her balance, her damp hand pressed to her cheek, her one thought was "It's over." Toshio was standing as if stunned.

"Go," said Tsuru, then. As he remained numbed by despair, she stared at him as if she would have liked to devour him. Toshio was crying with his mouth turned down like a child's. At the same moment that she slumped forward Toshio slowly turned away. The door closed gently.

A cry of "Toshi," then tears and violent sobs burst from her. She couldn't stay on her feet. Tsuyama's embrace was ready. She cried for a long time, taking comfort in the security of Tsuyama's touch as he stroked her back.

13

April passed, and May.

The trees lining the streets, like the one in Tsuru's dream, were dense with the green leaves of early summer. The freshness of the foliage brimming with new life reminded her of Toshio. Very soon the leaves would turn to hard, dark clusters under the June rains and the sun. Only in her vanished dream could new leaves remain new forever.

Her love for Toshio now seemed another dream. The memory was filled with expectations of lasting forever, an impossibility in the real world where young leaves soon change.

The love she hadn't wanted to lose had been a dream; only the lovers had been real. The love was gone, Tsuru still existed. And no doubt Toshio still existed somewhere. Like all who inhabit reality, they had both changed with time.

Tsuru had made no attempt to contact Toshio, and no word had come from him. This was the ending she'd already foreseen when he slapped her; it was even something of a relief.

Tsuyama had caught her in his arms as she'd reeled away from the love that had been a dream, and when she picked up the pieces of their old life together, Tsuru began to think it would have been senseless to throw it away. Tsuyama was, as she'd always known, an irreproachable husband and teacher. If he would have her, she resolved, she would spend her life with him. If she heard from Toshio she would tell him so.

In a corner seat at The Gendarme, Tsuru told Kanako of her decision. "I'm so glad. I really am," Kanako said with such emotion it might have been her own happiness at stake. "It must have been a tough decision."

Embarrassed, Tsuru looked doubtful. "Not really. People's feelings change naturally." It was a truth left her by Toshio. At this moment, she thought, Toshio—who'd been so afraid of a change of heart—might be drinking coffee somewhere, as changed as herself.

"You've always taken life too seriously, Tsuru. If you'd known as many men as I have you'd have developed some immunity. You wouldn't have come down with such a bad case."

"I'm not going to fall in love again," Tsuru said, ignoring her own reflections on the unpredictability of the heart. In fact she suspected she might, but next time she'd know better than to lose her head.

Perhaps that was what Kanako meant by immunity. Perhaps, she thought, she was now a slightly hardened leaf.

"I won't leave Sensei as long as I live."

"I should hope not. He deserves the best. I just can't tell you how distraught he was. I could hardly bear to see it."

"You think so? He seemed very cool to me."

"You were too head-over-heels to notice."

When Tsuru gave a wry smile, Kanako lowered her voice a little. "I couldn't have told you this before now, but actually it was Mr. Tsuyama who brought the news about you two. He came to see me and begged me to stop you leaving."

"What?" Tsuru felt the faint smile on her face stiffen.

Suddenly uncomfortable, Kanako said, "He didn't want you to know he'd been here. It wasn't easy for me, either."

A suspicion dawned on Tsuru—why hadn't she noticed before?

Kanako had said that she'd summoned Toshio for a talk, and he'd confirmed that she'd phoned him. Yet Toshio could have had no opportunity to give Kanako the phone number of his new apartment. And Tsuru certainly hadn't. Then how on earth did Kanako get it?

Only Tsuyama would have had ready access to the office records at the university.

Then Toshio had been right about the rumor, too: it had never existed. Tsuyama must have told Kimi himself.

She felt the letdown that comes on being shown the trick behind a simple conjuring feat—and the disgust at her own credulity. She hadn't noticed a thing. And all this time the giant eye had been in the most obvious place. What a laugh. She caught herself actually chuckling.

"That's a relief. I was afraid you'd be angry," Kanako said.

"Of course not. I owe you an apology for involving you in all these goings-on."

Tsuru's voice was so smooth and natural that Kanako relaxed further. "I was a bit surprised," she admitted. "I wouldn't have thought someone so mature would take it so hard. I did say to him, 'Are you quite sure? Are you sure you haven't been reading too much into what's happened?' And he said, 'No, I heard it directly from Tsuru. I've even gotten their conversations on tape.' And he showed me a cassette. Would you believe it, he'd been listening to your phone calls. That made my blood run cold, I can tell you."

For a second Tsuru heard no sound except the whir of something spinning in her head. The sight of Tsuyama stroking the blade of the silver scissors came back in an entirely new and lurid light.

"It shook me up. I'd always thought Mr. Tsuyama was one person who'd never stoop to a thing like that. He was really desperate to keep you, wasn't he? Poor soul."

The meaningless smile that had plastered itself on Tsuru's face made it difficult to breathe.

"The electrician's boy told me it's quite easy to tap a phone. And Mr. Tsuyama was always handy with electrical gadgets, wasn't he? Apparently all it takes is a small microphone attachment and a connection to a tape recorder. You never noticed anything like that?"

Barely listening to the rest of Kanako's remarks, Tsuru left The Gendarme as soon as she could get away. Her legs sped her home, the evening air rushing past her face and the street noise growling menacingly around her.

So he'd known. He'd known of her betrayal and her terror. Again and again the unperturbable Tsuyama bore down on her with each passing car, each pedestrian, and rushed on by.

Tsuyama, arriving home just as Kanako left and asking what she'd wanted. Tsuyama, informing Tsuru of the rumor he'd started himself. And, inevitably, Tsuyama knowing her dilemma as he took frequent pleasure in sex with her.

When she thought of the writhing, gnashing, mocking thing behind that unperturbable face, Tsuru was overwhelmed. The gently smiling woman who had thought herself a white bird in Tsuyama's eyes, who had trusted in the completeness of her own deception, had been a draggle-tailed fox. Tsuru felt each of her innards wrench with shame.

A harsh metallic taste filled her mouth as if she were about to be sick. She let out a long moan between clenched teeth.

Tsuyama had watched her as he might watch an ant's frantic scurrying on the palm of his hand. He had cleverly tilted his palm and made the ant run wherever he liked.

Rushing breathlessly into the house, Tsuru went straight to the study and did something she had never done in her life—ransacked another person's things. Tsuyama's drawers and cupboards were all unlocked, as Tsuyama held that privacy between them was a matter of mutual good sense. She turned everything out not caring about the mess, but what she was looking for didn't seem to be there.

She searched the bedroom, checked the living room, glanced over the tatami room, went back to the study, and then gave the living room another check. She ran to the shelf with a row of cassettes in full view and, though hardly believing it possible, pulled out the tapes of music and lectures at random until she came to three two-hour tapes which, unlike the others, had no neatly lettered labels.

She dropped one into the tape deck, whose location beside the phone had taken on a new significance.

Holding her breath, she waited for a sound from the speakers. There was nothing but static. Impatiently she advanced the tape a number of times. About twenty minutes in, a voice suddenly emerged.

"I can't stand it." It was strangely flattened, but definitely Toshio's.

"I can't, either." Her skin crawled at the sound of her own drawling voice.

"Next time I see you, wherever we happen to be—even if it's in the middle of the street—I'm going to kiss you madly."

"Mmm."

"You won't be embarrassed?"

"Oh, no. I might be the one to embarrass you by—"

Tsuru hit the off switch. She hadn't the strength of mind to listen any further. It was a conversation she remembered having had, there was no mistaking that, but what had then been heartfelt declarations of love had transformed themselves into ugly banalities she couldn't endure.

Tsuru hugged her arms and rubbed the goose pimples that had risen on them. When she thought of her husband listening closely to that same banal banter, the gooseflesh wouldn't go down.

By tricking and trapping them Tsuyama had destroyed their love; Tsuru was now past mourning its loss. A greater sadness had come with the knowledge that her husband had spied on her. The ideal of a decent, understanding husband had been shattered and with it, like the reflection in a mirror, the image of a devoted wife. However much she regretted the loss, there was no way to piece them back together.

It was her own fault, she thought, sitting hunched over and trying to console herself. If it hadn't been for her affair Tsuyama would never have been reduced to spying on her. He could have ended his days as a fine, understanding figure of a husband.

Though she condemned herself, she was unrepentant. The hopelessly ugly nature of what her husband had detected made it impossible to ask forgiveness. She could no longer judge which was true: the record provided by the tape, or that of her memory.

Whichever was true, the fact remained that her husband had eavesdropped on that ugly voice. There was only one thing left to do, she concluded after a long last look at the scattered fragments of the beautiful image of her husband and herself. It was simply not possible to go on living with Tsuyama now. Whatever he might have wished, all she could do was leave.

She got up quickly, shoved the three cassettes into her bag, and hurried out. The urgent need to leave allowed no room for sentimentality. As she did when running late for an appointment, she stumbled outside with her shoes half on, closed the door, and went through the gate—and there came to an abrupt halt.

Five or six paces away in the middle of the alley Tsuyama had also come to a stop. The two regarded each other in silence for a while. Tsuru saw with a new clarity the bewilderment and then anger that crossed his features beneath their stiff expression, and finally the pride that spread to conceal all. The thought that she'd never been free came suddenly to mind.

The wind blew in the fine evening sky. Fresh leaves rustled in the neighbors' gardens. Through their sounds she heard a voice: "Why shouldn't I fall in love?"

"I want a divorce," Tsuru said. She watched Tsuyama's face contort as he forced out a kind of groan: "Over my dead body."

For the first time Tsuru felt herself to be facing not her husband, nor her Sensei, but an ordinary man. This man was standing motionless like herself in the summer twilight. Her body grew light and her feet seemed about to lift from the ground.

"I'm sorry." With these quiet words Tsuru slipped past Tsuyama and flew away toward the broad street.

GOOD
AFTERNOON,
LADIES

THE STUDIO

Dust filled the vast box of the studio. In the space bounded by a high ceiling, which few except the lighting technicians ever saw, thick sound-absorbing walls, and a gray linoleum floor, the dust motes floated, neither rising nor falling but minutely changing places. Some of the dust had been in there for twenty years, ever since the studio had been erected on a foundation of guesswork and hope inspired by the amazing new technology that transmitted images as scanning lines. Some of the dust had flowed in only recently.

Settled at the bottom were the people.

People followed each of the three cameras—units more like self-contained robots than tools. People with cotton-gloved hands paid out the thick cables that snaked over the floor. Beneath the outstretched silver arm of the boom mike, people stood beside the monitors on wheeled stands and compared the small area under the lights with the screen displays of what they saw there. Under the concentrated lights people went through the motions of a conversation with partners not present. Among all these people still others came and went, some deliberately and some furtively.

There was no harmony in these actions. Yet they all knew that the camera whose light gleamed a warning red was spinning the scanning lines, and that in some measure their own actions were its materials. This shared knowledge created an invisible control among all the people there. Moment by moment they focused their awareness and centered their movements on the area displayed on the cathode ray tube. The slightest clearing of a throat in a corner of the studio came under this control.

The round impersonal face of the electric clock that looked down from the wall indicated 12:53, and over its pair of hands the red second hand swept steadily on.

The clock seldom told the kind of time that marked intervals in people's lives or their emotions. Its face showed time of uniform density and thickness, time that was consumed uniformly. This 12:53 was neither A.M. nor P.M. It did not measure the last few rushed minutes of a lunch hour, nor a lover's anxious moments of waiting. It merely calibrated the thirty seconds to be consumed before the next commercial break.

Beside the camera with its red light on, the floor director squatted like a Kabuki stagehand, visible but not visible. In his hand was a card reading "30 seconds" in large letters, which he flashed toward the team of announcers. The tall host who managed to look impeccably dressed in a loudly checked suit was flanked by two co-hosts, one in a pastel skirt and jacket with not a hair out of place, the other in a blue blazer and a little overweight. The host was directing at the lens the intimate smile that went over so well with the daytime audience.

"Well, that's *Stories from the Crime File* for today. Food for thought there for us, uh, hardworking husbands. And what do we have lined up for tomorrow?"

"Tomorrow we have our regular Tuesday feature, the series *Looking for Love*."

"Indeed we do, and we'll be taking up last week's—"

Listening with his uncovered left ear, the floor director replaced the card in the stack at his feet and, after a moment's pause that suggested he couldn't do it automatically yet, fanned the fingers of both hands and thrust them forward. In his right headphone he could hear the director's countdown coming from the control room, which overlooked the studio through a double-glazed window. His fingers relayed the cue-in in time with the director's digital clock.

Nine: left thumb. Eight: forefinger. Seven: middle finger. Six: ring finger. Five: little finger. Then four: right thumb. As he bent each, he thrust the whole arm out as if to drive forward all the seconds in the world. The anchor team bowed. The floor director bent his right little finger finally, then swung his fist down. Simultaneously a commercial for a food product appeared on the two studio monitors. Slipping the headphones down around his neck, he shouted, "Thank you." The same words were heard in various tones from the hosts, the guests, the cameramen, and his headphones. As control was lifted, the people in the studio, their time uncalibrated now, began to flow away in different directions.

A young man from an advertising agency cleared the detergent boxes from the set. The aproned young woman who did the flowers wheeled her wagon over to collect the vases from among the personalities, her attention distracted by glimpses of this or that famous person in the flesh.

The director of the day's show and a couple of his staff descended a steep metal staircase from the control room to the studio floor and joined the group on its way out. The director extended his thanks to the guests, suggested a cup of tea, and was engaged in conversation by the debuting singer and her manager. An earnest young staff member checked the guests' destinations and disappeared in the direction of the car pool.

The group streamed through first one then another pair of heavy doors and out into the corridor. A little of the enclosed dust crept out after them. The corridor, never seen as anything but a passage connecting the studio, waiting rooms, makeup rooms, and lobby, was uninviting. A battered aluminum ashtray on a tall, thin brass stand rested against the wall. Well, yes, it seemed to say, the place may be old and tattered, but the perforated ceiling hasn't fallen in, the walls are solid, the doors open and shut smoothly, the floor is level—what more could you want? Whoever designed the linoleum tiles had given the area its only decorative touch of marbled ocher and black.

Along this corridor the group drifted in twos and threes toward the lobby and its tearoom.

"Have you any idea how much sexism there is in the textbooks? The ones used in elementary and junior high schools?"

Toward the rear, an expert wearing three long necklaces was still hotly debating her fellow expert. When he grunted what could have been agreement or dissent, she pressed on, looking him intently in the face: "You really should read the pamphlet *Women Are Made This Way* put out by the International Women's Year Action Group. Read it and you'll see how school texts are still pushing a concept of women that's way behind the times even by conventional standards. It's appalling."

"But, you know, among my students it's the girls who act tough these days. The boys are the timid ones. Of course, I'm not saying that's wrong."

"Now just a minute. You can't go confusing a superficial phenomenon like that with the hard facts of sexism. You have to remember that even the most timid husband may well be exploiting his wife economically. I don't know whether you're a timid husband or not . . ."

Perhaps to take the harsh edge off her words, she laughed gruffly. Her fellow expert, whose graying wavy hair came down to his collar, said with a faint smile, "I'm happy to say that I'm the boss in my house."

"She's right about the textbook problem, you know," the director broke in diplomatically. He was walking close behind them with one of the co-hosts, Shichiro Ogu. "The other day my daughter had to circle the things that Mother does, and she was marked wrong for circling 'Going to the office.' "

"Ah." The woman expert nodded deeply as if to say the situation was only too familiar.

The director went on. "My wife does go to an office, you see. Our daughter told the teacher that, but—"

"Some of the textbooks have got it all mapped out, haven't they—Mother does the housework, Father goes to work, and to an office job, what's more." The woman spoke mournfully.

"Exactly. The teacher insisted the test wasn't at fault because it was based on the textbook, and besides mothers don't normally go to offices. That gave me a shock."

From behind them the psychologist who had been following their conversation overtook them and hurried on ahead, calling to the program host. "Mr. Hidaka!" Kazushi Hidaka, who was walking with his hand on the shoulder of his co-host Akari Kasai and leaning forward a little to talk to her, looked back without straightening up. Akari also looked over Hidaka's arm for the owner of the voice.

"I've been meaning to give you a copy of my latest book." As he fell into step alongside Hidaka, the psychologist was rummaging with difficulty through a bulging bag. On the outside a Playboy rabbit posed with a look as prim as its owner's.

"What, another book? You must be making big money. Is it right for a scholar to sell so well?"

Hidaka's ironic expression was dangerously close to the limits of humor, but the scholar took out the book between his stubby fingers without so much as a self-deprecating smile and extended it to Hidaka. "I only wish they *would* sell. It's not like one of yours, with sales of over a hundred thousand copies. That's why I have to keep on bringing them out." He chuckled as if this were very funny.

Finally removing his hand from Akari's shoulder, Hidaka opened the gaudy cover, handling it carefully enough not to hurt the scholar's feelings. "Well, well, you've even signed it. I'm very grateful."

Making a little bow as if he had stumbled on a stone, the scholar said, "Rather a good title, don't you think? *How to Create a Dropout?*"

Hidaka examined the book's cover again. "Hmm, yes. You've used it satirically, I see."

"Precisely. Mothers today may *appear* very dedicated to education, but they're actually having quite the reverse effect. Their efforts are only turning their children against studying. If they had an elementary knowledge of psychology they would never act as they do. I've covered the ground here in simplified terms."

"I must get my wife to read this. Our son is going to drop out any moment now."

The scholar chuckled again. "If you should happen to have the opportunity, a review . . ."

"Certainly. Won't you join us for a cup of coffee before you go?"

"Glad to. I have to wait for a car as it is."

As the group entered the tearoom in the corner of the entrance lobby, the floor director shouted from their rear, "Mr. Hidaka, Akari, Mr. Ogu. You'll be needed at two o'clock to discuss the arrangements for tomorrow. Screening Room B. Thanks, everybody."

THE VIDEOS

In the third-floor corridor on the way to Screening Room B, Akari said, "Does this mean we're going to watch that video again?" She glanced at Hidaka but he seemed lost in thought. Ogu replied from her other side:

"Oh sure. Koda just loves it."

Ogu always sounded bright and energetic; even when he was complaining or expressing his condolences, his voice never lost that sparkle. It was the sparkle with which the manufacturers of radio and TV sets had deluged the country, the sparkle that people who were cut off from the light demanded of television. It had got Ogu promoted from a run-of-the-mill local announcer's job to co-host of this show and brought him a modest increase in income and fame. He quietly enjoyed the satisfaction and the confidence born of this success and was, in fact, a bright young man in real life.

Akari's eyes widened. "He watches that video for pleasure?"

"I'm only kidding. Naturally he watches it because he's so involved in his job."

Before Akari could work out which of these was the joke, they'd arrived at Screening Room B. The door was open. Ogu, the last to enter, closed it behind him and sealed them in a small windowless room.

Though it was called a screening room, it had not originally been designed as one. Neither was it one of the VTR rooms that had been set up for sponsors and the press and studio executives when the equipment first came into vogue, along with video editing suites and libraries. It was simply a room containing a monitor plus tape deck in what must once have been part of the corridor or a staff room.

Here there was none of the scientific efficiency admired by visitors to the multistoried new administration block or the control rooms that could have belonged to a spacecraft. The TV with its tape deck was the only sign of the modernization that was going on in every living room. On the other hand, neither did the room have the raffish air of the studios, makeup rooms, wardrobe and prop departments that reminded one of an old-fashioned peep show. The dingy walls had absorbed neither skills nor labor nor history; the varnished lopsided table bore only the round marks of many cups and glasses.

The lounge suite—a sofa with a white cotton cover and two armchairs set formally around the table—had no doubt been inherited from some waiting room for studio guests. Yet it was in surroundings such as these, and in coffee shops and bars and other such places outside the building, that the people driven by relentless rationalization and revolutionary technology would struggle to come up with new program ideas.

Director Nobuo Koda was seated at one end of the sofa. As always his suit was an indeterminate dark color. He was tieless; the collar of his open-necked shirt, bordered with a row of navy-blue diamonds between two fine silken lines, was out over the collar of his jacket. A close watch would reveal that his jacket and trousers changed with the seasons and even from day to day in the same season, and there were times when his shirt would change from a white background to pale cream or even dark blue. People tended to believe, however, that he was always wearing the same outdated black suit and the same open-necked shirt with the collar out. Some four years earlier he'd had bifocals made and his reading glasses replaced, frames and all, but nobody had noticed. Despite slight changes in their shape, those black-rimmed spectacles seemed to have been as much a part of his face throughout his life as his eyebrows and nose.

Koda was leaning half of his medium weight on his bent left arm, which rested on the sofa's flat wooden armrest. His right hand lay palm up on his neatly aligned thighs. He made it a habit to wash his hands with soap at least five times a day. Seeing the three hosts arrive, Koda slipped his left hand from the sofa arm to lie palm up beside his right, and said "Good morning."

When spoken in tones as somber as his clothes, this didn't sound like the greeting that fast-living show business people—keepers of highly irregular hours—used at any time of the day or night.

In armchairs on either side of Koda sat two men. One half rose from his chair, then seemed to think better of it. This was the continuity director of the Tuesday series, sporting a flesh-colored suede jacket; his expression was soft beneath the lock of hair that fell over his forehead. Compiling the Tuesday show was a very simple job: Koda made all the decisions and he wrote them down. For this the continuity director was paid very well indeed compared with his previous program, a pop music show that had had him racking his brains for hours every week, after which he was still expected to pay the director a kickback. (The continuity director's job was a sought-after one.)

Working for Koda was for this very reason not entirely satisfying. To prove to himself that he was more than a secretary, the continuity director would occasionally make small suggestions of his own. These were generally adopted as long as they didn't run counter to Koda's own wishes. He sometimes suspected that the producer was keeping a continuity director on the staff merely to guard against budget cuts, and that his pay was only a small share of the money at stake; in this mood he would gaze intently at the credits rolling and be somehow reassured by the sight of his own name after the title "Continuity Director."

When these efforts failed, he reminded himself that he would not be a continuity director all his life. The job was a chrysalis—a cocoon clinging precariously to the branches of the studio tree till one day it would hatch the writer of a hit song lyric or screenplay, a best-selling author, or the kind of TV hero typified by Kazushi Hidaka, now settling himself casually beside the director. No doubt it was these feelings that had made the continuity man stop himself on the point of automatically giving Hidaka his seat.

The man in the chair on the other side of Koda looked like a sports-loving college student with his ample build and his woolen vest, white cotton shirt, corduroys, and thick rubber-soled shoes laced to the ankles. Unlike the continuity director, he rose immediately to his feet. As he added his own greeting to Koda's he was already on his way to fetch a folding chair from the stack against the wall and set it up for himself next to the sofa. He had been Koda's assistant director on the Tuesday show since the spring. Once everyone else was accommodated he took his seat.

Hidaka sat, legs lightly crossed, on the sofa beside Koda. His silk socks were visible between his slim Bally shoes with their feminine stitching and his good wool trousers of a bold mustard, green, orange, and gray check. Akari Kasai perched herself at the other end of the sofa where Hidaka had beckoned her to sit, while Shichiro Ogu groped in his blazer pocket for his cigarettes as he took the armchair vacated by the assistant director, and the continuity director finally made himself comfortable in his original chair.

"This is the script for tomorrow," said Koda with great formality as he handed each of the three hosts a book of mimeographed sheets in a cheap cardboard binding from the pile in front of him. The words *"Good Afternoon, Ladies"* danced in large letters across the center of the blue cover; above this title was the name "Kazushi Hidaka." Hidaka's name was listed again at the bottom with the other hosts, Ogu and Akari; in between were the words "Tuesday: *Looking for Love"*.

The print was very black and wet-looking, and indeed a little came off on Koda's fingers as he handed the books out. While he carefully wiped his hands clean and stuffed his handkerchief back in his trousers pocket, Koda said, "Are you ready, Mr. Kiyokawa?"

"Yes, any time you like," replied his assistant, on the point of getting up. Hidaka flipped idly through the pages of the book on his knee and said to no one in particular, "Do we really need to see the video, I wonder?" Akari looked up from her copy, first at Hidaka, then at Koda. Ogu shot Koda a quick glance as he exhaled cigarette smoke over the head of the continuity director, who was pretending to examine his ball-point pen. Koda leaned against the sofa arm as he had been doing when the hosts came in; he touched the frame of his spectacles with one hand and looked straight ahead, his expression fixed.

Hidaka closed his script and placed it on the table, then recrossed his legs and cleared his throat. His eyes turned to the screen as he continued. "It's not as if we've got a new one. It is the same one again, isn't it?"

"Yes," Koda answered. "I think we'd better take another look all the same. I'm sure you haven't forgotten anything, but it'd be best to run through it before I explain the new arrangements."

The continuity director knew this tone of Koda's well; when he used it there was no arguing. For an instant there was a dark gleam in Hidaka's eyes, but it was gone so swiftly that not even Akari, who was watching him, noticed. Hidaka turned to Koda offhandedly. "Right, then. Let's take a quick look." Then, giving the continuity director his slightly diffident smile that charmed so many people, he added, "I have been always inclined to cut corners, even in my continuity days. The directors didn't take at all kindly to it—you know old Seki?"

As Hidaka began to retell an almost legendary story involving a director who was now on the board of another channel, the continuity director—like all his colleagues—rejoiced in a sense of intimacy and warm admiration. Ogu, Akari, Kiyokawa and even Koda were entertained briefly by Hidaka's story.

"So I never could get on with an enthusiastic director. You must be having a hard time yourself, aren't you, with Koda?"

"No, Mr. Koda is very considerate." The continuity man grinned.

Hidaka leaned confidingly toward Koda. "Don't you believe it. In the dead of night he sticks five-inch nails into a straw doll with your name on it."

"That reminds me, Mr. Koda, didn't you mention you've been experiencing twinges lately?" This was supplied by Ogu. Koda joined the laughter with some reluctance, then turned back to Kiyokawa.

"All right, let's have the video, please."

"Yes, sir."

Hidaka folded his arms and sank back on the sofa. After a moment the picture appeared on the screen. It was a scene already shown twice on the program and everyone present had watched it at least four times.

*   *   *

For the first few seconds the picture was terribly unsteady.

A muddy color, then black, then white glare, then part of a body crossed the screen. When it finally stabilized, the right half was occupied by a man's back in a dark raincoat. His bobbing shoulders advanced down what seemed to be a narrow corridor. With each movement of his shoulders there was the squeak of floorboards that were none too sturdy. Also audible were other footsteps, clothes rustling, and something striking the microphone.

The man's back went out of focus as it came close to the camera. The cameraman dropped back and the picture sharpened. The top part of a door containing a pane of frosted glass came into view on the left. Glass and varnish glared under a hand-held light, fine scratches were highlighted, then vanished. The man walked on to the next door.

Nothing in the brownish picture had the tension of objects being filmed. Nor did the sounds picked up by the all-absorbing microphone have the tension of what is known to be overheard. A sour state of ordinariness—off-guard and shamelessly self-revealing—was recorded there in full detail.

The man stopped and showed his pudgy profile. The camera drew two or three steps nearer.

"This is it. Room 202. Yeah, this is it" came a mutter from the man's mouth. The camera rotated jerkily, then took in the door squarely from behind his neck. He glanced uncertainly off-camera a couple of times. Then there were three bursts of rapid knocking. The door filling the screen vibrated. Twice, three times, the door shook to the dull thudding sound. Over the last burst a woman's answering voice was heard from the other side, a muffled "yes." The man breathed hard.

There was a pause, then the muffled voice answered again but closer now, and at the same time the door opened a fraction. At once the man's back blocked the screen. Something crashed against the door. The picture wavered, searching for a way in. There was a scurry of footsteps. The screen cleared abruptly to show a woman from the waist up. She wore a pale pink nightgown, her brown neck sticking out from a lace border. The merciless lights plastered their oily glare over her collarbones, sallow unmade-up cheeks, and puffy eyelids. Several gaudy curlers protruded from a bulbous nylon nightcap.

The woman was looking around outside camera range, all color drained from her face. She stared at the lens and frowned suspiciously, then her eyes widened and she let out a wordless cry. Fending off the camera's gaze with both arms, she broke away to the left.

But a swift zoom out caught her full-length. She was standing doubled up with her arms over her face. At her feet could be seen part of a rumpled bright-blue quilt. The camera traveled down to where something was moving. It looked like a man's body in a sweatshirt, but he was partly hidden by the woman. Leaving him, the camera zoomed out again to capture as much as it could.

"Stop! Please, dear, don't!" The woman eyed the camera and the people around it between her arms, then tried to get out of the picture, her pink nightgown trailing pathetically.

"Don't give me that!" a man's voice roared, and at that moment the figure in the coat lunged on-screen. A hand grabbed his arm, only to drop back out of sight as the coat plunged toward the woman. The picture swung around. There was a violent smack and a woman's scream. Amid crashes and scuffling noises, the man hissed, "Made me look a real fool, didn't you? You bitch! Whore!" The camera eventually found the woman with the shoulder of her nightgown bunched in the man's fist. Red-eyed, she was holding together a rip in the neckline with both hands. Her nightcap dangled comically by her face, snagged on one of the red and green curlers that stuck out among strands of uncurling hair.

"Goddamn filthy slut." The man's hand struck her face.

"Stop! Please!" The sweatshirted figure tried to intervene.

"Leave her alone, you! She's my wife. What right have you got to tell me what to do, Kakimoto?"

"Stop! Please!" The man in the sweatshirt was followed by the camera as he scrambled away, shielding the woman at the same time. His underpants and the thin legs below them came into view. The man in the coat was close behind.

"You thieving little punk, I'll teach you to steal another man's wife!"

Just as the man in the coat hurled himself at the other man, who was attempting to shield the woman with his body and his own face with his arms, Nobuo Koda's voice was heard off-camera.

"Now, now, Mr. Yamashita. Mr. Yamashita, don't get emotional. Why not talk this over? Come now, Mr. Yamashita."

As the man swung another punch, a sturdy arm pulled him back. The screen went white.

"Hold it there, will you please?"

Koda had watched tight-lipped throughout, tucking in his chin and glowering up at the screen. Now he gave the order to Kiyokawa. With a sigh of relief Akari consciously relaxed the stiff muscles of her face and took the script in her hand. Hidaka, who had watched the monitor screen through half-closed eyes, was leaning back on the sofa making no effort to move. The continuity director jabbed his cheek with his ball-point as he lowered his eyes to the open script. Ogu surveyed the room as if wondering whether it was safe to crack a joke.

"As you all know . . ." Koda began, consulting his closely written notes, "at the request of Mr. Takao Yamashita, in our November sixth broadcast we asked his wife Fukuko, who had been missing since mid-October, to come forward. With the cooperation of our viewers her whereabouts were traced the same day, and on the seventh she was found in the company of Mr. Eiji Kakimoto. The video we have just seen shows what happened. Mr. Kakimoto is an employee of the bicycle shop owned and operated by Mr. Yamashita. Please refer to the summary of other relevant details on the last page. If I may just remind you of the following week's developments: after consultation with our panel of experts during the November thirteenth broadcast, a tentative solution was reached. Mr. Kiyokawa—"

The video started again.

Yamashita and Fukuko were facing each other. They seemed to be in the studio, for both they and their surroundings had the tension that indicated an awareness of being seen. Fukuko, in particular, was almost unrecognizable from the previous video. Though she constantly dabbed her nose with a handkerchief and her eyes were tear-swollen, she looked far younger than the woman surprised in her nightgown. She even looked beautiful. The picture, too, held still except when it cut to an occasional huge close-up; the irritating jerkiness had gone. Yamashita's voice now had an overbearing calm of which there'd been no hint before.

"Just think about what you've done. Don't waste time with your bawling. How many months is it?"

"Four," Fukuko answered in a small voice.

"Then there's no problem getting rid of it, is there?"

Pressing her handkerchief to her mouth, Fukuko shook her head. There was a close-up: every muscle was straining with the effort of holding something back. Yamashita's voice was heard.

"And you can count yourself lucky, too. How could you have faced the kids if you'd gone and had his bastard?"

The sobs welled up and tears poured steadily down Fukuko's face.

"Stop that bawling. What good'll that do?" Yamashita's voice grew angry. "I'm the one who should be crying. What a fool you've made of me. The whole neighborhood saw us on TV. The kids are upset and so's my Ma. They can't hardly walk down the street. It's all your fault and don't you forget it."

"That's over with now, Mr. Yamashita."

Koda's voice was heard. The picture returned to the couple facing each other. Yamashita looked around, past the camera, and smiled thinly. "So it is."

Then, his gaze reverting to Fukuko, he said, "Right then. It's all water under the bridge as far as I'm concerned. Now you're going to get rid of that baby and start over. Aren't you?"

Fukuko nodded again and again with a desperate vehemence. The screen went blank.

"Mrs. Yamashita entered the hospital in order to abort Kakimoto's child and make a new start. The day after the abortion, November sixteenth, she disappeared from the hospital with Kakimoto. Last week, on the twentieth, Mr. Yamashita made a second live appeal to Fukuko. Those are the developments to date."

Koda paused. Ogu asked a question:

"Where did they turn up—her and her man?"

He said "and her man" so easily that Akari darted a look in his direction.

"Kagoshima. Ibusuki."

"Oh? They really made a run for it, didn't they? They're quite something." Though he kept a straight face, Ogu sounded almost pleased.

"It seems they were contemplating suicide."

Koda stated this with due solemnity. Ogu responded brightly as ever: "They weren't dead, though?"

"No."

"I'm glad to hear it. No point in dying, is there?" Ogu sought Hidaka's support. Instead Hidaka turned his head toward Koda, keeping his arms folded:

"And so?" His tone was final. "I suppose it'll be the usual order? The discussion can be left to Ogu, and Akari and I will just do the summing up before and after?"

"Yes."

"What's the lineup for the panel?"

Hidaka picked up the script and turned a page or two. Going through his notes, Koda explained: "The five regular members, plus Mr. Kimio Hayami and Mrs. Kay Arlemois."

"Kay? Now which is she?"

"You know," said Ogu, "the beautician. Getting on a bit. A real tough cookie."

"Ah, yes." Hidaka placed the name. "She was on once before, wasn't she? Until I saw her I thought she was going to be a foreigner." With a grimace and a laugh he added, "I don't have a good memory for women over thirty."

Koda went on regardless. "I would have liked to have Mr. Toda, the principal of Sacred Star Academy, but he wasn't available this week. And Mrs. Kay Arlemois does have a great deal of experience of life. Though I must say there are certain areas in which one questions her common sense."

Hidaka nodded a number of times—enough to appear to be giving the matter his full attention. "She'll do. They're nicely balanced as a panel. I expect we'll have a first-rate discussion." This could have been the result of the deepest deliberation. The continuity director glanced equally at Hidaka and Koda as he made a mild comment:

"I expect so. I think Kay Arlemois will make an interesting contrast with Kojiro Sasaki among the regulars. Mr. Sasaki is very strong on the commonsense approach, isn't he? He's made it his trademark."

"Exactly. A debate's no good if they're all too similar. If Ogu manages things right, the discussion should turn out to be very interesting. And he's unbeatable at that. A true genius."

"Oh, come now, Mr. Hidaka. You can't be serious."

"I mean it. Everybody has to have *one* redeeming feature."

"I knew it." Ogu's offended look made everyone explode with laughter. Hidaka's "Well, then" coincided with Kiyokawa saying "Mr. Koda, I have to be getting along to Tokyo Station."

"Ah." Koda checked his watch on its black leather strap. "Mr. Yamashita is arriving on the 15:44 bullet train, isn't he?"

"Yes, sir."

"Go ahead, then. I'll take care of the other video myself."

Hidaka folded his arms and sank deep into the sofa. Kiyokawa departed briskly. Neatly replacing his sleeve over his watch, Koda turned to Ogu.

"When Mr. Yamashita arrives, I'd like you to have a few words with him."

"Certainly."

"We have a slight problem. Of the three parties, Mr. Yamashita and his wife Fukuko will be with us tomorrow, but Eiji Kakimoto will not. He has gone home, without warning, to his parents in Matsuyama."

"Oh, no." Ogu stared round-eyed at Koda. Observing with interest the anger struggling to find expression in Koda's features, he chose his words carefully. "Good grief. That *is* a problem. Can't we do something?"

"We know that he has definitely gone home to Matsuyama. But I'm too busy to go myself on such short notice, and he absolutely refuses to come to the phone. A member of his family always answers and says he's not in."

"In other words, he's abandoned the woman and gone home?"

"That is correct."

Koda gave the frame of his glasses a slight push, then with the same hand pulled out his handkerchief. Following these movements with his eyes, Ogu remarked, "Well, how about that?"

"However you look at it, Kakimoto is a key figure. Clearly he took the initiative in their second disappearance." The handkerchief passed from Koda's left hand to his right, wiping their palms in turn. His eyes, meanwhile, were studying a corner of the ceiling. His lenses gave them a strangely flattened look. His voice remained level and lackluster, but he was speaking a little faster than usual. "Hiding won't solve anything. That's not how a *man* behaves. It's the worst kind of cowardice. It's irresponsible, if you ask me."

Ogu knew exactly what he meant. "He's forfeited our sympathy, hasn't he?"

"Exactly. Initially we did receive two or three sympathetic comments from viewers impressed by Kakimoto's simple, down-to-earth manner. I've taken great care all along to consider his point of view."

Koda was clearly excited now; the face he turned to the anchor team was frozen and expressionless.

"Remember what he said during the first session? I intend to use that part of the tape tomorrow. . . ." He was half out of his seat.

"I'll get it." The continuity director took over and Koda sat back.

"Hmm." Hidaka pondered and reached a private conclusion. "Well, he's free to choose whether he appears on TV. Either way there should be no problem."

"But surely without Kakimoto we risk giving the impression that he's being tried *in absentia.*"

"Hmm. It's tricky, isn't it?"

"I wouldn't want to risk that."

"Hmm."

"However, we can't avoid bringing his name into the discussion."

"Hmm."

As he sat otherwise motionless, the toe of Hidaka's shoe was tapping rhythmically under the table.

An image appeared on the screen. Automatically all eyes turned to it.

*   *   *

The screen was filled by a man's face that had not entirely lost its childish innocence. Like a player on the team that has just lost the high-school baseball championship on nationwide TV, he was sobbing. He spoke haltingly, wiping his eyes with his arm from time to time.

"I'm sorry—to have caused so much trouble. Believe me—I didn't think. Please don't blame Fukuko. Please."

From offscreen came the blunt tones of Kojiro Sasaki, a regular panelist and TV personality who also covered nightclubs and massage parlors for the weekly tabloid press. His voice held a measure of sympathy. "Sure, it's hard on you. We can see that. But this is obviously the best solution."

The young man nodded meekly.

"Especially as Mr. Yamashita . . ." This was Koda's voice. "Mr. Yamashita has said he'll forgive and forget if only his wife will come back. Mr. Kakimoto."

"Yes."

"You'll commit yourself to part once and for all?"

"Yes."

The camera held for three seconds on his face fighting to hold back the sobs, and then the screen went blank.

Koda spoke. "This was recorded on the thirteenth and shown last week. By the sixteenth, however, he had made off with the woman straight from the hospital. And now, to crown it all, he's run out on her."

"Young people these days . . ." Ogu's murmur was the only response. Koda suddenly noticed the handkerchief in his clenched fist and put it slowly in his pocket.

"Okay." Hidaka sprang to his feet. He looked down at Koda, the script rolled in his hand. "You don't need me any longer, do you?"

"No, that'll be fine."

"Usual time tomorrow?"

"Yes. I'm counting on you."

Akari moved to let Hidaka pass. Once out from between the sofa and the table, he placed his hand lightly on her elbow. "Aren't you coming?"

Akari glanced inquiringly at Koda.

"That'll be all for now, Miss Kasai."

"Mind if I go out for a bite?" said Ogu, half rising.

"Go ahead. Provided you're back by four-thirty."

Taking the continuity director with him, Ogu was on his way. Hidaka had the door open and one foot in the corridor when he spotted an approaching figure. "Aha!"

"Hello there." The man stopped in the doorway and exchanged greetings with the others on their way out.

"Still hard at work?" Hidaka asked.

"Of course. I'm your typical company man."

"What, you? Our top producer?"

"Oh, come now." With a glance at Akari, Kenichi Tendo remarked to Hidaka, "Wish I was in your shoes. You're leaving, are you?"

"That's right," Beaming, Hidaka made a point of putting his arm around Akari. "I have a date with Akari. Eat your heart out."

"Now, you keep your paws off our precious mascot. Watch out, Akari."

"I'll be all right," Akari answered with a laugh and they went on their way.

Promptly dropping his roguish expression, Tendo called through the door, "Mr. Koda, can you spare a moment?"

"Yes," answered Koda from the end of the sofa where he still sat.

THE GUEST

Arriving early at Tokyo Station, Kiyokawa downed a bowl of noodles in a basement cafeteria, then went up to the bullet train platform ten minutes before the train was due. It was chilly on the platform, but the view was bathed in a gentle light. The mostly grim-faced crowd hurried by, sat on benches, read newspapers, and jostled around the kiosks. Kiyokawa stood erect and gazed past them all at the sunlit scene, whistling an almost soundless tune. It vaguely resembled his college rugby club's song.

In his first three years with the channel, before being made Koda's assistant, he had been assigned to a quiz show and a talk show. Neither had interested him, and the same went for *Good Afternoon, Ladies.*

If he had to be in production at all, he would have liked to work on dramas; otherwise he would much rather have been transferred to sales where the real businessmen were.

He had taken the job at the TV company not out of any great desire to make programs but simply through a connection of his father's. He had wanted experience in a different line of work before joining his father's firm, and when his father had recommended the TV company, he had jumped at the chance. It had such a modern image. And besides—he had thought, with a youthful attraction to the arts—it might be fun to have a shot at directing dramas and things.

He had been far too optimistic, as he quickly learned.

He was allocated to production and not administration. He had indeed become a corporate employee, but his job would hardly be relevant later, as his father's firm dealt in the simple buying and selling of goods. This job was a strange mixture of pure manual labor and physically taxing mental work. There was little hope, either, of getting into the drama department that had tickled his artistic fancy.

Some studios still produced their own dramas in quantity—ten or more a week—but most relied largely on made-for-television samurai and detective movies shot elsewhere, as it didn't pay to make more than three or four dramas of their own.

Indeed, the company he had joined was the one cutting back most heavily. Of the five drama slots each week, up to four were now filled by TV movies and it began to seem as though the remaining one served only to keep the production team employed. He had heard rumors that it, too, was to be canceled.

But although this had given him second thoughts about the job, he was not unduly disappointed. He would always have an escape route. He planned to stick out the ten years he'd originally given himself, before he was due to join the family firm. He was trying for a transfer to sales, where he could deal in the commodity known as programs. Meanwhile, he made the most of this assignment in his own way. In any case he enjoyed the physical work. Regardless of how he viewed the job, he had an aptitude for it, and since his elders—at the studio as elsewhere—liked the sort of discipline acquired on the college rugby team, he was treated with affection by the senior staff and known to them all as "Dai"—big—not only because of his size and his large eyes with slanting brows, but also because Daisuke was his first name.

Koda, too, had taken an immediate liking to him, or so it seemed, although he alone insisted on calling him "Mr. Kiyokawa." Kiyokawa saw this as punctilious rather than cold.

He left off whistling the club song as the train was announced. Soon the beetle-faced superexpress slid into the terminal with a shuddering roar, cutting off the sunny view, and came to a stop.

There was no sign of Takao Yamashita in the appointed car, but he was the first to step from the rear door and survey the platform.

When he spotted Kiyokawa running up and calling his name, he raised his hand in a friendly wave. "Ah, thank you."

"You must be tired. Let me take your bag."

"No, no, don't worry. I'm traveling light—not expecting to be here long this time." As he spoke, Yamashita handed over a black imitation leather travel bag. They mingled with the moving crowd.

Yamashita was a man of medium height and build, one of many in the crowd. His heavy face featured slack deep-red lips, eyes set into dark lids, brows that almost met in the middle. The top of his head was balding. He wore a dark coat and walked with a sway as he swung his short arms. Though it wasn't so obvious when he was on his own, alongside Kiyokawa he looked a terribly mousy little man.

Yet there was no trace of the wretchedness, the pathetic ridiculousness that must have struck anyone who saw him appeal to his missing wife from the TV screen. He now had the manner of a city dweller at home in a crowd, alert and lively enough. Kiyokawa noticed his thin hair had a self-conscious neatness as if freshly cut. Perhaps that was why he looked like he'd put on a little weight. Kiyokawa couldn't keep his eyes from straying to Yamashita's clothes as the unbuttoned coat parted with each step he took.

They were very different from what he'd been wearing last time— then he'd dressed just as frowsily as a neighborhood bike shop man might be expected to. Now he had on a suit that was plainly new, even if it wasn't tailor-made or of good quality. It was of a synthetic pongee silk in a clear gray. Over a freshly laundered shirt he wore a tie of a strange shiny material patterned with fine red lines intersecting on a bright blue ground.

Having just seen him in Screening Room B, Kiyokawa couldn't help recalling the brown sweater with the drooping turtleneck and the stiff, dusty gray-green cardigan that Yamashita had worn while berating his wife.

"We go straight to the studio, don't we, Mr. Kiyokawa?"

Kiyokawa hastily took his eyes off Yamashita's clothes.

"Yes, Mr. Koda is expecting you."

"This place is as crowded as ever. Ah." Yamashita stopped in front of a kiosk. "Mind if I have something to drink?" He mimed putting a can to his lips. "It was hot on the train all the way up. Gave me a real thirst. Only thing was, I was right out of change."

"Oh, of course. What'll you have?" Kiyokawa went up to the kiosk rather more briskly than he'd intended, counting out the coins from his pocket.

"A beer," Yamashita replied. On being handed the cold can, he gulped it there beside the kiosk, out of the rush of passersby. Kiyokawa hung around and waited. Lowering the can and wiping his mouth with his hand, Yamashita commented, "Aha, our good friend Sasaki Sensei is on the ball, I see." Following his gaze Kiyokawa saw a rotating book stand; among the titles displayed was *Kojiro's Adult Playgrounds*.

"I read an article of Sasaki Sensei's in a weekly magazine. Said there's some very unusual nightspots at a place called Horinouchi." Yamashita disconcerted Kiyokawa by pushing his face close with a knowing look.

"Oh, yes?"

"You haven't been there?"

"No, I'm afraid not."

"Pity. I was hoping you'd show me around."

He tilted the can again, then wiped his mouth. "And here I am all dressed up specially. Like it?"

With his free hand Yamashita held his coat open, pivoting to give Kiyokawa the full effect.

"Very nice." Kiyokawa thought hard and added, "*Très chic.*"

Yamashita gave an embarrassed laugh. "Thanks. I figured a lighter color would look better on TV."

"Ah."

"It will, won't it?"

"Yes, you're quite right."

As Yamashita upended the can again, Kiyokawa's eyes wandered uneasily to the passing crowd and back.

"Who sells better, Hidaka Sensei or Sasaki Sensei?"

"Hmm." Kiyokawa had no idea. "I'd say it was Mr. Hidaka, wouldn't you?"

"He must be rolling in it."

"I guess so," Kiyokawa said with a wry smile.

"Wish I had half his luck. Me, I work, work, work, and never get ahead. And then my wife goes and runs off with another man. Twice."

This was a subject that made Kiyokawa nervous while they were alone together. He consulted his watch with a broad gesture and was about to hurry Yamashita along when, having emptied the can and tossed it into the bin at his feet, he got moving on his own. "Sorry to keep you waiting."

Picking a taxi which would accept the company's voucher, the two headed for the studio.

THE DIRECTOR

"It's only the ratings surveys that keep me in television." So producer Kenichi Tendo had stated in a magazine interview. "Whether good or bad, they're an incentive. They're half the fun of working in television."

Kenichi Tendo had displayed outstanding acumen as a producer since his early thirties. He had come up with a large number of hit shows, and he enjoyed seeing his talent clearly demonstrated by the ratings. To him, these figures whose fluctuations baffled his colleagues were the scores in a game the principles of which he understood very well.

When he put his mind to improving them, eight or nine times out of ten the ratings went up. If they went down, he would examine the situation from this angle and that like a mechanic checking over a car, and invariably the cause would come to light. Unlike a car, however, the situation was constantly changing. He had to adapt his methods from season to season, moment to moment. And so he was never bored. It was even more fun than the tests he'd taken in his student days. The sight of his colleagues agonizing over their ratings was as puzzling to him now as his fellow students' agony over their tests had been then.

While he was playing this game, he had rapidly moved up at the studio and gained increasing power. This earned him the respect of the advertising agencies and the performers' agents. His talent lured sponsors and enriched the advertising agencies. His talent and power launched entertainers and, with luck, made them stars and the agents rich. They arranged for Tendo to profit in ways that were not always entirely aboveboard. In fact, most of the people who made their living through television supplied him with benefits of one kind or another in order to benefit themselves.

His monthly paycheck was not spectacular, but Tendo never wanted for spending money; he had acquired a fancy house where his wife and children lived while he himself was more often out in his Ford Capri. Of course, there was much speculation and gossip behind his back. There were constant scandals involving women. But nothing could eclipse his talent and his power, nor his charm, which worked on men and women alike. Nothing could touch his career.

It was Tendo who had revived the flagging *Good Afternoon, Ladies* show. After studying the competition on other channels, he had advocated Kazushi Hidaka as host. At that time—five years ago—Hidaka had begun to make his distinctive mark as an essayist and critic. The two had been close friends since their early days at the studio, and Tendo had assessed Hidaka's abilities and character with the eyes of a producer from the start. Ignoring the general opinion that he was a bit too much of an intellectual to appeal to the daytime audience, Hidaka had rapidly overtaken the competition to rank high on the housewives' Top Ten of the most attractive men, and *Good Afternoon, Ladies* for the first time had a fighting chance of becoming the most popular show of its type.

Who should do what to boost the ratings? Here Tendo was astute enough to give the series *Looking for Love* to Koda. At first this had no effect. Then in the fourth week the Tuesday program moved to the top with a 2 percent lead. At once the other channels launched similar series. These were successful up to a point. As the competition grew tougher, however, Koda's series went on surging ahead, and today, two and a half years later, it held a 10 to 20 percent lead not only over the rival shows but over all the series that *Good Afternoon, Ladies* featured on other days of the week. Although the 12:00 to 1:00 time slot could command a regular audience of only 5 or 6 percent, rising to 11 or 12 on a good day, *Looking for Love* obtained a steady 20 to 28 percent.

It was Tendo's belief that just one thing made the difference: he had Koda and the other channels didn't.

"When you think of the extent of television's influence, you must agree that it's absolutely essential we should codify our ethics."

"Oh yes, yes."

Tendo, in a quiet suit no less smart than Hidaka's, reclined without lounging in an armchair and regarded Koda with clear eyes, nodding his agreement. When this well-built man with his sculpted features just a little short of perfection responded in this fashion, anyone would have the gratifying sense that they were being listened to.

"Of course, they must be ethics, not biases. The code must always be fair."

"Yes, indeed."

Watching this subordinate of his, three years older than himself, Tendo reflected that it was entirely because of this man that Tuesday had such amazing ratings. As always, Koda seemed a strange creature in Tendo's eyes. Not that he didn't understand Koda. On the contrary, the better he understood him, the more he sensed that here was a creature completely unlike himself, that if he himself were a human being, then this was some weird alien species.

"That is why I always value the viewers' opinions and do my best to interpret them correctly."

"What you mean is you don't follow the viewers blindly."

"Precisely." Leaning forward slightly, Koda continued. "The modern age is afflicted by a lack of ethical standards in society at large. Naturally the general public, and thus our viewers, suffer from the same problem. It would be a crime for television merely to give the public what it wants. Isn't it time that television with its immense influence took the lead and made a stand for morality? This will require courage. Such a stance is unlikely to find favor with the intellectuals. No doubt the laissez-faire libertarians will be particularly vocal in their opposition. And yet—I believe this stance is the only correct one. Am I wrong?"

After a moment's thought, Tendo said, "No, I think you're basically correct."

"Yes. In that case, for the sake of television's future, surely it's admissible—and even desirable—that this stance should be made clear?"

"Boldly, without fear of criticism, you mean?"

"Yes, boldly and without fear of criticism. And that is why—" Koda thumbed through a notebook. "Er, in regard to the present matter, if we exclude the payment to the detective agency—would you mind taking a look at these?"

Koda slid along the sofa, laid the open notebook on the table, and pushed it across to Tendo. It was a large, narrow-ruled book densely filled with columns of small writing. Tendo sat forward and glanced over the notes. They made up a simple logbook:

Oct. 30—Mr. Yamashita to Tokyo. Decision to begin investigation.
      Mr. Yamashita returns to Osaka.
Nov. 4—Fukuko and Kakimoto's hideout located: Karinso Apartments, Nakano.
Nov. 5—Mr. Yamashita to Tokyo.

Nov.   6—Live broadcast. (Mr. Yamashita appeals to wife.)

Nov.   7—Early morning visit to Karinso with Mr. Yamashita, Kiyokawa, and three-man crew. Fukuko and Kakimoto agree to appear the following week.

Nov. 13—Live broadcast. (Fukuko and Kakimoto decide to separate as result of discussion.)

Nov. 15—Fukuko enters Ebara Maternity Hospital in Setagaya. Has operation.

Nov. 16—Fukuko and Kakimoto abscond from maternity hospital. Followed. Detective agency takes over at Tokyo Station.

Nov. 17—Known to be in Atami.

Nov. 19—Known to be in Ibusuki.

Nov. 20—Live broadcast. (Report of second disappearance, Mr. Yamashita's second appeal.) Contacted at night by detective who has prevented double suicide and is to escort them back. Mr. Yamashita returns to Osaka in the evening.

Nov. 21—Fukuko and Kakimoto to Tokyo. Meeting. Kakimoto does not agree to appear on following week's program.

Nov. 22—Second meeting. Kakimoto again refuses.

Nov. 23—Kakimoto disappears without notice from Hotel Eight, Shibuya. Fukuko safely at Mitaya Inn.

Nov. 24—Unable to contact Kakimoto.

"According to my records, we have met the following expenses: Mr. Yamashita's round trip on October thirtieth. Sixteen days' accommodation and round trip for the period November fifth to the twentieth. That makes the total for Mr. Yamashita roughly 110,000 yen to 120,000 yen. For Kakimoto there's just the fare between Ibusuki and Tokyo and then two days' accommodation. For Fukuko, eight days' accommodation from November seventh to the fourteenth and the fare from Ibusuki to Tokyo, plus accommodation for the—five days, is it?—since then. And in her case there are the

50,000 yen hospital costs. I don't have the exact figures in hand, but I'd say the total comes to about 220,000 yen altogether."

"Yes, I've been given the general picture."

"Then there are Mr. Yamashita's three fees for appearances on the program and one each for Fukuko and Kakimoto. Also—I believe it was the day after the November thirteenth broadcast—Kakimoto came to me in distress, saying he couldn't go home. I arranged for him to receive around 70,000 yen in the form of a payment for assistance to our reporting team. I hoped it would help him get his life back together again. Having involved ourselves already, in my judgment we couldn't in all conscience have turned our backs on him."

"That was very considerate of you, Mr. Koda. If he'd come to me, I'd have told him to grow up," Tendo said seriously, then broke into a smile. "I'm sure you never dreamed he'd use the money to run off with the woman a second time?"

Koda bridled. His eyes flicking to the blank TV screen, he said slowly, "No. He betrayed my trust." Tendo lit a cigarette. Its smoke drifted heavily past Koda's face. The stiffness went out of Koda's back. "I can assure you," he continued, dropping his gaze to the surface of the table, "these expenses were incurred in an ethical manner. We would have nothing to be ashamed of if they were to become known."

"I'm sure that's so." Tendo let out a puff of smoke along with the words. "Mr. Koda, I think your stance—boldly and without fear of criticism—is a rare and precious thing. That is, *I* personally think so. But I wonder if the world is ready for it?" Tendo was watching the burning tip of his cigarette. Koda was watching the same spot in silence. "What I mean is this: no matter how right you are, if you take your stand at the wrong time you'll be annihilated. I'd say that society at this time will reject the social good you're calling for. For instance," Tendo turned a mild gaze to Koda, "the hospital and surgery costs for Fukuko Yamashita. I expect you took care of everything out of a sense of responsibility, the station having already become involved?"

"Absolutely. Fukuko and Kakimoto couldn't have paid. Mr. Yamashita insisted on Kakimoto paying. Unless somebody took care of it, the solution we'd so carefully worked out would have come to nothing."

"But the press will see it this way, won't they: a TV station forced a woman to have an abortion. And the public will be more receptive to that explanation than to your own. That's the way things are these days. And then there's the 70,000 yen you handed Kakimoto just two days before he and Fukuko disappeared again. I simply can't see people keeping those two things separate in their minds. If people decide that the TV station gave them a nudge in that direction to liven up the program, do you think for one moment that they'll stop to listen when you say it was the considerate thing to do?"

Koda was staring tight-lipped into space.

"To accomplish anything, even when your ends are valid, you need strategy," Tendo continued calmly. "If we relied on the missing persons always being found for us we could never plan ahead. Naturally the investigation must come first. And as we can't do it all ourselves, sometimes the investigation may even get ahead of the program. That's only natural, too. However, if the public heard that we'd known the missing couple's whereabouts since November fourth but publicly appealed for information on November sixth, there's only one way they'd see it: the station concealed the couple's whereabouts and made the husband go through the ordeal of appealing, all to create a better program. The same applies in Ibusuki."

The flesh under Koda's chin was creased into two thin folds as he drew it sharply in. There was a silence.

"I must say, though," Tendo changed his tone while casually taking up the notebook, "what a coincidence it was that you happened to arrive at the hospital just as they were leaving. It *was* a coincidence, I presume?"

Koda was wiping his palms with the handkerchief that had appeared in his hand.

"Yes, of course. Actually, what happened was that Kiyokawa telephoned me the night before and confessed that he'd inadvertently told Kakimoto the name of the hospital."

"Oh? Dai did?" Tendo's eyes very faintly lit up with an expression of amused interest.

"I had made him promise earlier to keep it quiet, but from what he tells me he wasn't entirely to blame. After receiving the money I'd arranged to pay him at the studio, it seems Kakimoto went for a drink with Kiyokawa. At Kiyokawa's invitation. He's a sensitive young man, as you know, and Kakimoto had impressed him initially as a decent type. So when Kakimoto broke down and cried, and Kiyokawa had had too much to drink, it seems Kiyokawa got carried away and before he knew it he'd revealed the address."

"Really? Dai did?" Tendo repeated with an air of great amusement.

"He was most apologetic. The next morning—actually it would have been around noon—I thought I'd better go and check that all was well at the Ebara Maternity Hospital, and just as I arrived—"

"They were leaving."

"That's right."

Koda pressed the rim of his glasses with the hand that gripped the handkerchief.

"I was shocked and horrified. What a monkey the man had made of me! After he'd sworn to end the affair—that was why I'd arranged the money. And Fukuko—running off like that! A woman with three children. The eldest is fifteen. One can only think she's sex-crazed. Depraved. Television must never condone such immorality."

"Oh, I didn't realize how late it is. I have to take a sponsor out at four-thirty."

Tendo ran his eye down the notebook once more and said, "I see." He closed it and, hefting it a little as if testing its weight, went on: "I say we keep all the detailed expenses under wraps for a little longer as we always have done. The same goes for the investigation. No one is to mention it. You'd better warn Shichiro Ogu. Not the others—we don't want to bring it up needlessly, it'll only have the wrong effect. And the business with Dai, and your having followed the couple, must be kept strictly confidential."

"Very well."

Tendo put the notebook in Koda's hand, got up, walked to the door, and wheeled round. "Whatever the outcome, this case is to end tomorrow."

With rare agitation Koda leaped to his feet. "But—"

"Getting into a rut is the worst thing we can do. You've located the next missing person, haven't you?"

"Yes, we do have two other investigations completed. But—"

"Good. At the end of tomorrow's show, schedule an appeal for one of them." Flashing a smile, Tendo turned to go. Koda came after him.

"But we won't have time to bring them to the studio—"

"If they can't make it, have them phone the appeal in. Hidaka can look wonderfully sad on the end of a phone."

Tendo laughed aloud. Koda closed the door properly and, as he walked down the corridor behind Tendo, said, "Actually, Fukuko Yamashita is in rather a bad way."

"Oh, really."

Tendo's pace didn't slow.

"She was asking to see you."

"Really."

"I'm planning to call in at the Mitaya myself later on, but I wonder if you could spare the time to stop by?"

There was a pause.

"I'll go," said Tendo.

THE MASCOT GIRL

Across the gently curving counter the bartender waited for orders, his private thoughts wrapped up in a smile and polished manners. Arrayed behind his back with even more polish were rows of variously colored and shaped bottles and glasses, and then a clear glass wall. Beyond it there was a clear sky over which evening had not quite spread, and below that the streets of Tokyo.

"A vodka gimlet for the young lady. And make mine . . . a gin and lime."

Hidaka gave the orders without consulting Akari. That was his habit when out with a woman. He was confident of anticipating her tastes in choosing the place, the time, the drinks, the menu. None of the women refused his choices. This was because he generally guessed right, and even when he was wrong they didn't complain, not wanting to spoil the evening. Hidaka went on anticipating women's tastes with calm confidence and took pleasure in his skill.

"Tokyo looks pretty good from up here." He spoke in a murmur so quiet he might have been talking to himself rather than to Akari, who was perched on her stool and looking out of the window as if unaccustomed to such things. Then he chuckled and rested his chin on his hand. "People are scurrying about down there in all that clutter. Kind of petty, isn't it?"

Compared to human potential, all daily activities were petty. Beside the grandeur of the spirit all daily emotions were small-minded. He always liked the view from the forty-fifth floor because it was a clear reminder of these easily forgotten facts. And the public with its annoyingly persistent way of plucking at his sleeve couldn't reach him here on the top floor of a luxury hotel standing on a hill. That was another reason why he favored this spot.

Being a star, Hidaka was at home in high places.

Like all stars of whatever era, Hidaka was strongly colored by his times, by the same colors that all men wore inwardly or outwardly.

The skepticism of those whose boyhood faith in their nation's military destiny had been betrayed by defeat. The unconditional freedom that rose like a rainbow over the postwar chaos. The democracy that took on the rainbow's hues. The hope of reconstruction. Economic growth and the resulting "happiness." Living with the mass media. While these conditions had made most men's lives little better, if not actually worse, to Hidaka and a handful of others they had imparted particular talents and a particular kind of personality, then propelled them to fame and fortune.

The times had treated Hidaka especially kindly. He was a continuity director when television was first flourishing. His pop song lyrics went straight to number one, riding the crest of the booming economy. He debuted as an essayist with a lightly satirical style that breathed freedom and democracy to the delight of a public sated and disenchanted with the "happiness" of economic growth. And the crowning success was his popularity on *Good Afternoon, Ladies*.

When asked to comment on his success, Hidaka would always dismiss it as "luck" and give his disarming smile.

The bar at the top of the luxury hotel also allowed him to savor his luck.

"You're early today," said the bartender as he worked.

"Ah." Hidaka checked his watch. "Decent citizens are still at work, I suppose."

The bartender grinned.

"What luxury—drinks with a pretty girl before the sun goes down. I guess I'm going to seed."

As he efficiently set their glasses in front of them, the bartender commented, "I envy you."

"I hope this isn't poisoned?"

They had had this same conversation many times before from start to finish, but the bartender answered as slyly as he had the first time: "Well, I won't guarantee it." Adding "Especially when you're in the company of such a beautiful woman," he neatly saved

Akari from feeling excluded. Hidaka drew back as if only just noticing Akari's presence. "You think so?" He pretended to stare. "Hmm. She does have a shapely nose, but her mouth is on the big side. And her eyes could be a shade closer together, couldn't they? That light makeup suits her." Hidaka's appreciative gaze took in all of Akari in her plain dress and white mohair cardigan, but all he said was "She does have more style these days." Then he added, "I wouldn't call her a beauty. But she's not bad, not bad at all. What do you think of yourself?" he inquired.

Akari had been glaring laughingly at him. She pondered for a moment, then said, straight-faced and in measured phrases, "Sometimes, I think I'm hideous. Sometimes, I think I'm a great beauty. Right now, I don't know."

"You're a strange one." Hidaka burst out laughing. "Most girls would say either 'What a question!' or 'I've never thought about it.' "

Following Hidaka's lead, Akari raised her glass to her lips. She tasted, nodded, and took another sip.

"How is it?" Hidaka said confidently. "Like it?"

"It's excellent. What was it called?"

"A gimlet."

"Oh, yes. What was it I had before?"

"Before?"

"You know, dr—dram something."

"Drambuie?"

"Yes, that's it."

"You had one of those, did you? You're going to seed yourself. When was that?"

"You remember—I'd been on the show about three months, so it would have been at the end of last year. When you took Kako and me to dinner in Akasaka."

"Ah, yes, so I did."

Hidaka had a faraway look as if casting his mind back ten years.

"Now that you mention it, this is our first real date together, isn't it, Akari? I wonder why I didn't ask you out sooner." Surprised at himself, he turned to her. "Such an attractive young lady."

Akari answered with an easy laugh. "Oh, but you've got so many girlfriends. And Kako will never forgive me. Though lately I'm not so sure."

Hiding an odd little smile from Akari, Hidaka took a sip before speaking. "I haven't heard a word from Kako. Any idea what she's doing?"

"She's fine. Says she's going to get married as soon as she leaves college next year."

"Oh?"

The odd expression returned to Hidaka's face.

"It's funny about Kako," said Akari, looking at the darkening view outside.

"What is?"

"She had such a crush on you. It's because she was such a Hidaka fan that I ended up on the show."

"Is that right?"

"Uh huh. She replied to the ad to get closer to you. And she not only applied for herself, she filled out applications for me and all her other friends. Oh, but—" Akari looked blankly at Hidaka, who at that moment was nodding as if it was coming back to him. "Didn't I tell you about this at the interview?"

"And you were the only one they asked to see, right?"

"Yes. She was so overjoyed, she came along to my interview. But—" Akari looked perplexed again. "I'm sure I told you this after I joined the show, when I introduced Kako to you."

"Did you?"

"You don't remember what other people have said, do you?" She sounded honestly puzzled.

Hidaka laughed rather uncomfortably and said simply, "I'm not very interested in other people. . . . And then?"

"Then?"

"You were telling me about Kako."

"Oh. Well, as I was saying, she had a terrific crush on you. She didn't waste any time, did she?"

"No. She was quite something."

"Then, after a bit it was as if she just suddenly lost interest. And now she has a crush on someone else. Seems she intends to marry him." Akari gave a little laugh. "I like her the way she is—I'm not sure why, but it appeals to me. All the same, I really don't understand."

His expression mellow, Hidaka said, "Weren't *you* interested in getting to know the famous Kazushi Hidaka?"

"No, I wasn't."

Hidaka smote his forehead and pretended to reel, gasping "Such brutal frankness." A year ago she would have been startled, but now Akari only chuckled.

"It wasn't like that at all. I mean, I wouldn't have had a hope. It would never even have occurred to me. You were a celebrity, you belonged to a different world. I'm not like Kako in that way."

"And now? I don't belong to a different world now, do I?" Hidaka leaned toward her.

"Well, I don't know."

"Why not?" Hidaka seemed to be enjoying himself very much.

"To tell you the truth, I don't really understand you."

"All right then, I'll explain whatever you want to know. Go ahead, ask me."

He looked up smiling and nodded to the bartender, indicating his empty glass, then returned to Akari without waiting for the response.

"You're forty-six, aren't you?" she asked.

"Uh huh."

"You know, you're not at all like my father, even though you are the same age."

"What!" Hidaka looked genuinely shocked. Then he started to laugh. "I suppose we would be. My eldest is in her first year at college, after all. I really could be your father. Why did you have to remind me?''

"My father is awfully straitlaced—I guess it's because he's a high-school teacher—and he seems old already. I can't imagine him going out with women like you do."

"What do you mean, 'like you do'?''

"How shall I put it?'' As Akari searched for words, Hidaka suggested archly:

"Adultery? Immorality? Fornication? Licentiousness?''

"Is that what you're like?''

A new glass was placed in front of Hidaka. Taking a sip, he shook his head. "Don't get me wrong. It's true that I'm intimate with a lot of women. I admit it. It's because I love women, I love sex, I'm a very sensual man. I admit that, too. But I put my heart and soul into an affair and I never let a woman down. Each one is very important to me. I never treat a woman badly."

"But you go to hotels with girls you've just met, don't you?''

"What's wrong with that?'' Hidaka looked amused.

"Nothing, I suppose, but is that what you call heart and soul?''

"Listen, Akari, I don't buy women and I don't rape women, either. What we do is by mutual consent, all right? Sometimes it's just once and I don't even know her name. Sometimes it turns into a long, long affair. But the point is that I take good care of her always and make sure she has a good time. That's what I mean by heart and soul. What could have more heart and soul than that?''

Hidaka had put his case persuasively. After further thought Akari said, "Then you don't fall in love?''

Hidaka's laugh was explosive. "That's a good one, Akari. Very good.'' Catching his breath, he went on. "Yes, I fall in love. That's how I see it at any rate. Yes, I'd call it falling in love. For example, I look at you and I think, ah, you're very attractive, resting your elbow on the bar like that. And then I start to wonder what it'd be like holding you. I want to touch you, and already I'm falling in love. You don't agree?"

Akari answered thoughtfully, "I don't think love—real love, I mean—is as convenient as that."

"Convenient?" There was a hint of self-mockery in Hidaka's tone. "Give me convenience every time." Then he frowned slightly and put the glass to his lips.

"How about your feelings for your wife?"

"I love her deeply," Hidaka answered promptly. "She's everything to me, in fact."

"Then what about the other women?"

"I love them, too, at the time," he answered, and snorted with laughter. Akari laughed, too.

"That *is* convenient. But I really don't understand, you know." She began to look thoughtful. "I wonder if Kako prefers convenience?"

A little dryly, Hidaka inquired, "Has Kako been talking?"

Akari said innocently, "Has something happened?"

"You little—" he said happily, giving her a playful box on the ear. "Go away. Hurry up and quit. Next season I'll pick a woman who's better looking and better behaved." And he stuck out his tongue.

"You'll just have to put up with me for another ten months," Akari replied.

It was the policy to change the woman co-host on *Good Afternoon, Ladies* every two years. This was one of the simplest ways of keeping the program fresh: the newcomer would be featured in the entertainment news, and would revive not only the viewers' interest but that of the program's producers (all of them men), in whose eyes women were best when new, like the proverbial wives and tatami mats.

"What are you planning to do? Will you stay in television? Or get married?"

"I'm not sure yet. I don't expect to get married for a while. The way things are going, I'll have to repeat a year at college. I don't want to get married while I'm still a student, and anyway there's no one I want to marry. I enjoy working in television. But when it comes to staying on, there are too many things I don't understand. . . ."

"You don't understand a lot of things, young lady." Hidaka's tone suggested he'd found her too much of a handful but wasn't going to let it break his heart.

In September of the previous year the publicity department had issued a press release:

"From over 500 applicants, Kazushi Hidaka and the *Good Afternoon, Ladies* team have selected Akari Kasai (20). Born in Tokyo on June 17, 1959, Akari is currently a student of oil painting at the Women's College of Plastic Arts. She was judged ideal for the program because of her blend of old-fashioned good breeding and contemporary sparkle. At 5'3" and 106 lbs., the slender Akari radiates wholesome vitality. 'I'm thrilled and nervous at the same time. I don't know a thing, but I'm the curious type so I think I'll get along all right. This is such a rare opportunity. I'll try to learn as much as I can and live up to everyone's expectations.' With her screen debut scheduled for the first week in October, Miss Kasai is ready to go."

Unknown to Akari, the actual number of applicants had been more like two hundred, and of the thirty-odd who were interviewed, many had not formally applied but knew someone at the TV company or were backed by an agency.

All the same, Akari had blushed confusedly when she saw a small item based on the press release in a weekly magazine. For the first time she was gripped by a sensation to which the professionals had become inured—or could do a passable imitation of having become inured in order to remain professional. What she felt was the reaction invariably aroused in the real thing when it encountered the false image.

Never mind that they'd got her birthday wrong (it was the eleventh) as well as her weight (it was *110* lbs.). What struck Akari was the overall impression that the article created. She couldn't say it was all lies, but somehow it wasn't the truth. She couldn't put her finger on what was wrong. Whatever it was, there was a horrible clash between this version and what she'd actually thought on finding herself launched into a job on television—of all things—by a friend's impulsiveness and her own curiosity.

Before Akari found any solution to this mystery, a rush of new experiences overwhelmed her. Her days were full to bursting. She absorbed knowledge from the various situations covered by the program, and even more from the people who produced the program, and her curiosity grew. As one small problem was solved in her slowly revolving mind, another would arise in its place, while things that she thought she'd solved reappeared as part of a bigger problem again.

"Are you happy with the Tuesday show?" Fingering the stem of her glass, Akari looked for a reaction from Hidaka. He returned her look with eyebrows raised as if to say he hadn't understood the question.

"Personally," she continued, "I can't stand it."

"Oh?" Hidaka barely nodded, then folded his arms and made no further reply.

"At first I had no feelings about it one way or the other," Akari went on. "Of course I was startled when people cried and quarreled in the studio, but back then everything that happened startled me. Perhaps that's why I didn't feel anything much. And, anyway, I don't think it was as bad then as it is now. We used to do the appeal once and follow with one panel session or two at most, and that was the end of it, wasn't it?"

Hidaka's eyes lingered on Akari's shoulder as he listened closely.

"And the cases—I remember quite a few straightforward cases of runaway children. And the videos weren't so shocking. At least, I didn't think they were at first. But since this spring . . ." Akari broke off and sipped her drink as she recalled the scene. "Remember that man with amnesia we had on in the spring?"

Hidaka thought a little. "Yes, I remember."

"Ever since then, the program has been getting me down. Mr. Koda brought him to the studio, remember? His brother and his mother were waiting. They ran to him in tears and called his name, but he just stood there. He'd lost his memory, right? Mr. Koda and his brother sat on either side of him and showed him film clips and talked at him and asked him over and over 'Don't you remember?' until I couldn't bear it. It was horrible to watch him trapped there between them.

"It was obvious he was getting more and more confused as they tried to force his memory. He was fidgeting and turning red. I was on edge myself. And yet Mr. Koda, who could see what was happening, didn't ease up at all. In fact, he went on grilling him even harder.

"Then suddenly the man started to shake. You saw it, didn't you? It was as if there'd been an explosion inside his body. Even his chair rattled—you could hear it all through the studio. And still Mr. Koda didn't stop. Maybe it only lasted a minute or two until his doctor stepped in, but to me it seemed more like an hour."

Akari was staring out over the city where a few early lights were coming on, as if she could see the man's trembling figure out there.

"I still dream about that man trembling. I hear the chair rattling, too."

"Amnesia is a form of self-defense. The mind senses danger in certain memories and blocks them out. If you try to force the person to remember, his defenses will only get stronger," said Hidaka, but he seemed to be thinking of something else.

"I wasn't sure we ought to be doing that to him. Then gradually the show began to concentrate more on runaway husbands and wives—especially wives. It became our standard method to barge in on people and film them in a panic. Whenever I see one of those videos now, I wonder whether we really ought to be doing this. All sorts of things bother me now that never bothered me before. Those close-ups of the wife in tears, for example—we put her on nation-wide TV looking terrible. And all those very private details of their marriage that we make public. I feel I'm doing something wrong. I used to be able to tell myself we were helping to find missing people. But when I look at the latest programs I just don't know what in the world we're doing. I hate it.''

Akari waited, but there was no answer. Hidaka's fingers beat time to the background music on his folded arms.

"What can Mr. Koda be thinking of?" she asked. Hidaka gave her a sharp look.

"Shall I tell you why he insists on showing that unbearable video?"

"Please do.''

"He wants to give us a dose of the obscene morality that his own head is stuffed full of. He wants to shove it down our throats. The dirty rat.''

Akari looked closely at Hidaka.

"What's wrong?" he said, only his mouth softening.

"I didn't realize you felt like that.''

"Let me tell you, his type makes me puke," Hidaka said, relishing every word.

"Mr. Hidaka, your table is ready when you are, sir." The dark-suited maître d'hôtel was at his elbow speaking in a murmur. They moved through to the restaurant there on the forty-fifth floor.

THE ARRANGEMENTS

After parting with Tendo, Nobuo Koda returned to his desk and as instructed contacted the next people who had asked to make an appeal. One who lived in the Tokyo area agreed to appear the next day. At once he arranged for a car to be sent in the morning, wrote out the background details and a description of the missing person, delivered these to the graphics department for conversion to titles and display panels, then contacted the private detective agency and directed them to confirm the whereabouts of the missing person and place a round-the-clock watch on the house.

Koda was one member of the team who never cut corners. He personally saw to things that other directors would gladly have left to their staff. This had not, however, brought him success or promotion. In his entire history of nearly half a century, the *Looking for Love* series was his only achievement of note. For the first time he was in the limelight. There he continued his methods, cutting even fewer corners than before.

After pausing for breath, he phoned each member of the counseling panel to confirm the next day's schedule. When that was done, he withdrew to the small reception room attached to the production department and while awaiting Takao Yamashita's arrival reworked the arrangements for the next day, comparing the script with his notes.

Shortly afterward, Shichiro Ogu showed up at 4:30 on the dot, and ten minutes later Yamashita was ushered in by Kiyokawa.

"I can't thank you enough for all you're doing." Yamashita stood bowing in the doorway, then was seated, his coat on his knee. Ogu ran his eye interestedly over Yamashita's brand-new suit. On Koda's instructions Kiyokawa left the room to order coffee and tidy up a few small items of business.

"You must be tired?" Ogu inquired in a friendly way.

"No, don't worry. The trip's nothing now that I've gotten used to it," Yamashita answered quickly and leaned toward Koda. "So they were in Kagoshima?"

"That's right."

"And now?"

"We've put her up safely at an inn."

"She's not going to run off again?"

"Don't worry, Mr. Yamashita. Relax. The proprietress is keeping an eye on her."

"Yes, but . . ." Yamashita moistened his lips and gave a thin smile. "You told me not to worry the other time, too, Mr. Koda—when Fukuko was in the hospital."

Koda bristled. "The situation is different this time. When I told you not to worry then, I believe I was referring to the medical care being given your wife? You yourself weren't worried about her disappearing again at that time, were you?"

"Well, no, but I was only going by what you told me. I trusted you, Mr. Koda, and left her entirely in your care. And she ran out on me again. So it's no wonder I'm worried. I've been burned once already."

"Mr. Yamashita," Koda said loftily, "you make it sound as if *we* had burned you."

"I didn't mean it like that." Yamashita pulled back, startled.

"Who was it who ran away? Who was missing? *Your* wife. And you wanted her found. You do remember? You were most insistent."

Yamashita nodded and fumbled with his coat.

"At your own wish we offered our cooperation. As for the hospital, you'd never have coped with the situation at all if we hadn't taken care of it, would you?"

"I know, and I'm grateful," Yamashita said meekly.

"I must ask you to keep one fact very clearly in mind: when there's a problem with the wife, half the responsibility lies with the husband. This incident is, to put it plainly, partly your own fault. If you forget that and turn upon those who are cooperating with you in good faith, you're making a mistake."

Its quietness gave Koda's voice a kind of authority. He added the softness he might use to reason with a child. "Mr. Yamashita, since the second disappearance you have the sympathy of both the viewers and the counselors."

The coffee arrived. When the cups had been passed around and the waiter's check signed, Ogu said as he spooned sugar into his cup: "I can see it must be a worry for you, Mr. Yamashita, but . . . well, wouldn't it be better to let us worry about your wife while you think about how to handle the discussion tomorrow? That's the important thing, after all."

"That's true."

"How do you feel about it now?"

"As far as I'm concerned." Yamashita paused, holding the spoon in his cup, and looked at Ogu. "As far as I'm concerned, nothing will undo what's happened." He continued stirring, not watching his hand, then stopped again. "I've had my name dragged through the mud twice. I've had my home and my business wrecked. In the old days they'd have both been drawn and quartered, wouldn't they?"

"Well, yes," Ogu answered seriously.

"I want that understood. I'm the victim here." He glanced at Koda. "Yes, a husband is responsible for his wife. But I'm the victim and make no mistake. I've been cheated by her and by Kakimoto, too. I want the whole country to know what they're like, the pair of them. But before I knew what was going on, on the last program I was made out to be the bad guy who'd come between them and stood in the way of true love."

"That was very much the minority opinion, Mr. Yamashita," said Koda.

"Some of the panel sounded like they were on their side. That makes me look pretty silly."

"But as I said, this time they'll have formed a different impression."

"Yes, indeed," Ogu put in. "Surely it's better not to be too emotional. Everybody's well aware that Mr. Yamashita is the victim. But when they see him on the warpath they're bound to sympathize with the people being attacked. It's human nature. Don't you think so, Mr. Koda?"

"Yes. It would be better if you stated specifically what you expect your wife or Kakimoto to do about this intolerable situation."

"What—" Yamashita studied Koda's expression for clues. "What does she have to say for herself?"

"She says she doesn't want to return, but she's merely being stubborn if you ask me. Kakimoto has abandoned her. She has no choice."

Pursing his lips and staring into space, Yamashita gave a number of small nods. Then he said with obvious distrust, "Is it true that the little rat's gone back to Matsuyama?"

Ogu laughed. "Why would we want to lie about it?"

"No, I didn't mean that. . . ." Yamashita gave an ingratiating smile. "It's just that there's no telling what that shit will do," he added, and sipped his coffee. Koda looked at his watch.

"Tomorrow will be another heavy day, so perhaps you'd better get some rest in your hotel room. We'd like you to have your own proposals as definite as possible before we go on the air."

"All right." As he hastily got up, Yamashita asked, "Er, if we don't reach a proper settlement tomorrow, will you have us on again?"

"Let's discuss that after the program."

"I'm ready to go all out for what's due to me." Yamashita's loose mouth twisted momentarily. "You'll have a great show."

Koda rose without answering and called Kiyokawa, who had returned to his desk. With repeated bows to them both, Yamashita left Koda and Ogu in the reception room and went out with Kiyokawa.

"He's losing his innocence, isn't he?" Ogu's delighted comment drew only an unwilling smile from Koda.

"There are one or two things I want to make clear, Mr. Ogu."

Ogu straightened up. "Yes, what are they?"

"I've decided on short notice to put in a new appeal tomorrow in the slot before the ending instead of continuing the discussion. I'll give you the information in the morning, and we can go over the details then."

"All right."

"One other thing. It's a minor matter, but please be sure not to mention the particulars of Fukuko's hospitalization and the circumstances of the disappearance that followed."

"Ah." Ogu's face took on an odd expression. "You mean who made the arrangements with the hospital and how Kakimoto came to know where it was? I don't know much about it myself."

"That's right." Koda carefully took off his glasses and pressed the bridge of his nose with his index and middle fingers. "It's not that we have anything to hide. It's only that it's a complicated matter and once we brought it up there simply wouldn't be time to deal sufficiently with the background."

"Time, yes, I see. So in the course of the discussion I should make sure we don't get bogged down in too much detail."

"That's right."

"Will do," Ogu replied energetically.

THE PRODUCER

After his meeting, Kenichi Tendo turned down the sponsor's invitation to the Ginza and headed for the Mitaya, an inn near the studio. Hearing him decline the invitation, the advertising agency's man had teased him:

"There must be a woman waiting."

"How did you guess? She's waiting at an inn—a married woman I've only met briefly once before," Tendo had coolly said, then shook his head and added, "People are strange. Women especially. All women are utterly unpredictable to me."

Tendo slipped in through the Mitaya's gate, the only one with a small lighted sign on the quiet back street behind office buildings and apartment blocks both large and small. He let himself in and stood waiting in the highly polished entrance hall. After some bustling inside, the proprietress emerged through the split curtain in a plain but smart kimono of Oshima silk. "Oh, Mr. Tendo, we haven't seen you for a while."

She knelt on the darkly gleaming wooden floor, the movement revealing her age—she was over sixty—in a way that her youthfully smooth features did not. The Mitaya had been there longer than the television studio. Back when the studio was built and its staff began to use the inn for parties and work sessions, the present proprietress's mother had been in charge. The old woman had died over five years ago.

"I've been neglecting you." In his younger days he'd often stayed there with Hidaka (then a continuity director) and the team compiling a program, or come over to join a mah-jongg game, or, occasionally, to spend the night with a woman, but now that his spheres of work and play had broadened he hardly ever made use of the Mitaya. Even so, the proprietress, being accustomed to dealing with the TV people, wasted no time on needless pleasantries. "You're here to see the studio's guest?"

As he took off his shoes Tendo murmured assent.

"Mr. Koda mentioned you'd be coming."

"Is he still here?"

"No, he left about a quarter of an hour ago."

After neatly aligning Tendo's shoes, the proprietress straightened up and said, "It's depressing having a guest like that." She put on a look of deep gloom. Tendo responded to her familiar manner with his old form of address:

"Sorry, Ma."

The woman smiled. "What worries me is the thought that something dreadful might happen. Mr. Koda warned me very strictly."

"It's only till tomorrow. Please be patient."

"Oh? Only till tomorrow?"

Brightening up, the proprietress led the way down the cool corridor to a secluded room at the back of the inn. Having first sent her away with an order for beer, Tendo announced his presence.

"Come in, please."

As he opened the sliding door he put on a smile. "How are you feeling?"

The room could almost have been designed as a prison. The only exit was the door that Tendo had just opened; although there was a window alcove in the wall to his right, behind its shoji screens there was a pane of glass in an aluminum sash and behind that were narrow wooden slats, while outside lay a small courtyard with clustered rocks and plants. Set into the wall on the left was a closet for bedding and beyond it a perfunctory tokonoma alcove. The only furnishings were a black writing table over by the far wall near the tokonoma and a small mirror stand by the window. The spotted red-and-white cloth that covered the mirror and the single yellow chrysanthemum in the tokonoma did their best to add warmth to the atmosphere.

Physical warmth came from an electric heater beside the writing table. The woman sat leaning against the wall between the heater and the mirror stand. In her hand was a straight-sided glass one-third full of amber liquid. When she saw Tendo she placed the glass on the tray by her knees and edged away from the wall, drawing her legs under her in the formal way. She clasped her hands as if to wring them, bowed her head to him and kept it down.

"I heard you'd asked for me." Tendo spoke in a low but cheerful voice as he sat cross-legged, his back to the closet, on the cushion that must have been provided for Koda.

"I'm sorry to bother you. You must be busy." The Osaka accent gave Fukuko's low voice a supple softness. Her hand made a move toward the glass and paused.

"Go ahead. I've just ordered a beer."

"My nerves are on edge," she said apologetically as she picked up the glass, but she only looked at the liquid between her hands. These carried the marks of long years of housework in the red wrinkled knuckles and the torn skin around the nails. But her lips were shapely and when she closed them a dimple appeared in one cheek. Her eyebrows curved cleanly above nicely shaped eyes. Her hair, which had lost its perm, fell over her forehead and set off the paleness of her skin. Perhaps it was only the smallness of her nose and the sagging under her jaw that made her look ordinary. After a while Fukuko took a long sip, blinking as she swallowed.

"What did Mr. Koda have to say?" Tendo spoke in the same tone he might have used in a brightly lit coffee shop.

"Several things. He told me to pull myself together. Said I'm not a child and I can't go on dreaming forever. It's true. There I was, thirty-nine years old, still dreaming a stupid dream." Fukuko's eyes were on the fine silver threads woven into the dark green borders of the tatami mats. "I guess you've got to do your dreaming while you're young."

Tendo stroked his chin lightly and answered, "Nonsense. Thirty-nine is still young."

Fukuko slowly shook her head.

"Age doesn't come into it. When a woman has three children she's old."

Tendo was looking this way and that around the room, noticing the layout and the furnishings.

"Then he told me to go back to my husband. Mr. Koda always tells me that every time we meet. I understand what he's telling me very well. But . . ." She broke off and sipped her whisky. Letting out a sigh, she went on. "I thought I'd better talk to you, Mr. Tendo."

For the first time she looked timidly at him. Tendo turned his handsome face directly to her and, returning her look with twinkling eyes, asked, "Why me?"

The proprietress announced herself at the door and, sliding it open, brought in beer and appetizers on a tray. Tendo said lightly as he drew it toward him, "Thanks. Oh, Ma, we'd like to have a talk undisturbed . . ." and concluded with a nod to the proprietress.

Once the door had closed behind her, he chuckled as he poured the beer. "You're an unusual person."

Then he raised his glass for a moment to Fukuko, drained the dainty amount it held, and tilted the bottle once more. "Why me, I wonder? I believe we've only met once, with Koda."

"Yes, at the TV studio."

"And what's more, we hardly spoke."

"No, we didn't."

Fukuko put her hand to the side of her face and rubbed her palm across her forehead. "Perhaps I'm not quite right in the head after all that's happened. The day I met you was the day I went into the hospital. I was waiting at the TV studio for Mr. Koda to take me there. I was waiting by his desk while he finished some work. I was in such a state then, I hardly knew whether I was alive or dead. The people moving about before my eyes could have been in a movie, and the sound of their voices seemed to be coming from very far away. That was when you came up to us, Mr. Tendo. You talked to Mr. Koda, then looked over at me and said, 'You've had a run of bad luck, haven't you?' "

"Was that what I said?" Tendo smiled.

"Yes, you said 'You've had a run of bad luck.' I don't remember much else. But it was when you said that right off, and so cheerily— all the people and voices around me suddenly came up close again. Until then, all sorts of people had said things to me, both hard things and kind things. But you were the only one who said cheerily, 'You've had a run of bad luck.' That's it, I thought, it was bad luck. That's what it was. And once I thought of it like that, I began to feel I was going to make it through."

"And was that why you tried to run off again?" Tendo asked with interest. A faint smile spread over Fukuko's face.

"Looks like when you're out of luck, you can't do anything right. I only thought I could make it. When I tried, it soon went wrong."

"They tell me the two of you attempted suicide?"

"If you can call it that. Last Tuesday they put out another bulletin about us on TV, didn't they? I didn't see it myself but I could tell by the change in people's attitude at the inn where we were staying. We knew at once they were onto us, but we'd run out of money and were trapped. We decided we'd have to get away from that inn at least, and late that night we sneaked out. We were just walking along with nowhere to go when we came to the beach. We did talk about suicide. But I'm not sure that either of us really meant it. We just kept walking up and down by the water, saying to each other 'We could kill ourselves.' 'That's all there is left, isn't it?' 'That's all there is.' Then suddenly the detective from the studio came up and stopped us, and we gave ourselves up. So in the end we were so weak we couldn't even kill ourselves. The same goes for Yamashita."

Tendo was looking at the dainty glass he was twiddling between his fingertips.

"When I met you, Mr. Tendo, I suddenly had the feeling I could make it through. I thought if I could see you again today I might be able to get a grip on myself. I don't like weak people. I want to be strong."

"I'm sure you can, from what I know of you."

"How?"

"Well"—Tendo breathed a small sigh—"that I can't say. I'm not a part of your life."

Fukuko took a long swallow from the glass. When she lowered it the level had dropped noticeably.

"If it'll make my husband feel better, I'll go on TV as often as he wants. The way I see it, however many times I have to go through that it can't be helped. But Eiji is sick and tired of it. He's gone and left me. And now—I know it's strange, but I don't miss him anymore. The only feeling I have for him is a sort of fond memory. I can hardly believe that we really eloped together. And, you know, I already felt that way long before he left me. I felt that way all the time we were on the run after I had the operation. Then why did I leave the hospital and stick with him all the way to Kagoshima? I really don't know.''

"Everybody does something they can't explain once in a while.''

"Now that he's gone I needn't ever have left home. That much is clear to me. And after all we've been through—'' Fitful laughter bubbled up and made Fukuko break off. "After all we've been through, there's nothing left. It's really very funny. I think to myself, what have I been doing all this time?''

She brushed the corners of her eyes, wetting the backs of her fingers. "Mr. Koda is right. I really ought to go back to my husband. There's the kids and the housework and helping with the business. It's better than nothing, I know, but still I can't do it.''

"It gets on my nerves just watching someone like you.'' Tendo's calm manner seemed to belie his words. "If it's better than nothing, why don't you go ahead and make up your mind?''

Fukuko lowered her reddened lids. "You're a strong person, aren't you, Mr. Tendo? I'm not.''

"What lies.''

Fukuko raised her eyes in surprise at his teasing tone.

"You must be strong—you're a woman. I've never met a weak woman yet. What gets on my nerves is hearing someone who's really strong making excuses to herself about being weak. Go straight back to your husband and be happy with the life you have. If that's what you think best.''

Fukuko shook her head. "A man can't understand. If it was only going back to the house it would be easy. But going back would mean—being Yamashita's wife.''

"Yes, it would, wouldn't it?''

"He says he'll let bygones be bygones. But it's hard to forget a thing, isn't it, once you know it? I don't think he's going to forget that I went to bed with another man. I won't be able to forget it myself. Even if he acts as if nothing happened, I'll always be aware that he knows. Every time I see his face I'll be reminded that I was unfaithful to him. And I'll spend the rest of my life watching my step, trying to guess what sort of mood he's in, afraid he's going to bring it up again. I couldn't stand it."

Tears streamed down Fukuko's cheeks and dripped to her knees. Saying "Silly girl," Tendo reached out and wiped the tears from her chin. Fukuko cried aloud and threw herself against him like a slender stem that has been struggling to stand alone and finally falls before the faintest breeze. He held her with one arm, the hand lightly stroking the back of her head as it pressed against his chest. "Shhh. Qui-et-ly," he hissed as if they were playing hide-and-seek; he stretched his free hand behind him and strained till his fingertips just reached the door and clicked down the small catch on its frame.

"It's simple," Tendo said. His hand had returned from the door catch and was stroking Fukuko's back. "You don't want to spend the rest of your life feeling you're in the wrong, do you? That's because you don't really feel you *are*. The problem will be solved if you put yourself genuinely in the wrong. I'll help you."

Fukuko raised her face questioningly and at once Tendo placed his lips on hers. She didn't resist. It was a long kiss. Taking his lips away, he whispered, "See, what'd I tell you? You are strong. You do what you want."

Fukuko was looking up at Tendo's face, close to hers, with a confused expression.

"This'll put you genuinely in the wrong with your husband, and he'll never know. Even if he pesters you over the business with Kakimoto, you'll only have to remember tonight and you'll be able to stand it easily. If you know that you've actually been *more* unfaithful to him than he thinks, you can stand anything."

As he spoke, Tendo's hand methodically undid the ribbon on Fukuko's blouse, then the buttons, and made its way inside. She stiffened and said breathlessly, "Someone might come."

"It's all right. The proprietress has a lot of sense."

As she slid down onto the tatami mats, Fukuko murmured, "How come you're so strong?"

PLAYBACK

As Koda had instructed, Daisuke Kiyokawa had dinner in Shibuya with Takao Yamashita. Of course it was at the studio's expense. Though Yamashita kept hinting that after the meal he wanted to be taken somewhere sleazy, Kiyokawa managed to get him installed in an inexpensive hotel instead, then turned his steps toward his favorite bar.

This was a small place in Aoyama staffed by its owner and one girl, but its style and relatively low prices were popular with an image-conscious clientele of limited means. The production people from the studio often gathered there.

The counter was topped with black plastic, the tall stools consisted of thick brass pipes topped with black vinyl upholstery, the three cubicles across the aisle were furnished with seats of thick foam rubber and black vinyl, the tables were of brass and thick glass sheets, the wall-to-wall carpet was shaggy and gray, and Buffet reproductions hung on the white walls. Perhaps this heavily black-and-white interior was restful to those who worked daily with a dazzle of colors.

Since first coming here with a colleague shortly after he joined the station, Kiyokawa had taken to dropping in two or three times a month. He seldom drank very much. If he met people he knew, he enjoyed a good talk; if he was on his own, he enjoyed the peace and usually went home when he'd had just enough.

But events on this night took a turn that was neither enjoyable nor peaceful.

On entering the bar he was about to sit at the counter when he was hailed from the furthest and darkest table. "Dai, over here."

It was Nakazawa, director of the talk show on which Kiyokawa had previously worked. He was drinking with one of the technical crew, a man five or six years Kiyokawa's senior. Once he'd joined them, Nakazawa offered him whisky from their bottle and asked, "Are you managing to not screw up these days?" As he spoke his hand strayed to his fine paisley scarf at the neck of his white shirt.

"Yes," replied Kiyokawa politely, nodding his head.

"You were terrible at first, weren't you? He was too shy to give the cue signs clearly. There he was, fumbling away. I couldn't make out why we weren't getting started so I yelled from the control room, 'The cue! The cue! Daisuke, the cue!' Then from my headphones comes Daisuke's voice like a mosquito whining. 'I've given it, but they're not taking any notice!' "

The two men laughed loudly. Kiyokawa, red-faced, laughed a little.

"Afterward I gave him a crash course. I got him out in the middle of the studio and took him over and over it—'Now, go on, no, that's hopeless, do it again.' " Nakazawa seemed happily drunk. "Are you giving the cues so they can see them these days?"

"Fortunately I'm not on the floor anymore."

"Oh?" Adding ice and whisky to his own glass, Nakazawa asked, "And how is Maestro Koda?" He tilted his face inquiringly toward Kiyokawa; its small inverted triangle had slightly protruding eyes and a large nose.

"I've been learning a good deal from him."

"Don't give me that preppy stuff."

Kiyokawa smiled wryly and sipped his whisky. "To tell the truth, it's easy being assigned to Mr. Koda. He does everything himself, you know? I don't have to think much, just follow orders."

"I hate that," the technician said.

"It can be frustrating, yes. But watching Mr. Koda, I'm impressed. He takes the job seriously. He works very hard, doesn't he? He never settles for second best. I'm always aware of how much there is to learn from him."

"Huh." Nakazawa drew his own conclusion. "You've got a problem. You're too naïve."

"Stupid, in other words?"

"No, I wouldn't go that far. But you shouldn't be so impressionable. Think of the show he's making."

"You mean *Looking for Love?*"

"That's right. What's he playing at?" Nakazawa crossed his legs and twisted sideways, looking askance at Kiyokawa. "That program's a scandal. It's a flagrant invasion of privacy, a vicious attack perpetrated in the name of television. You think it's pretty good, huh, Dai?"

"No," said Kiyokawa in confusion, "or at least I'd never thought of it in those terms."

"That's what I meant by naïve."

"I don't think it's outstandingly good. If I had the choice I guess I'd rather not be involved in that kind of thing. I don't personally want to interfere in other people's quarrels. And if the studio were stepping in to sort out people's personal problems without being invited, I wouldn't approve. But a lot of requests come in for searches. From people whose wives or husbands or whatever have run out on them. They're in bad trouble."

"So you're cooperating and helping solve their problems? That's Koda's rationale, you know."

Kiyokawa looked from Nakazawa to his grinning companion. "You don't agree?"

"Never mind, go on," Nakazawa said.

"All right. So what if Mr. Koda does do it to help people? There's nothing wrong with that, is there?" He studied Nakazawa's face.

"What about the missing ones, then?" Nakazawa asked. Kiyokawa drank his whisky and frowned a little. Watching him, Nakazawa added, "They're happy where they are, and then next thing they know they're being tracked down and dragged into a TV studio."

"It may seem unfair, but Mr. Koda doesn't accept everything the relatives say. We do a very careful preliminary investigation. And the search only goes ahead in those cases where it's judged to be in the best interests of both parties. I know of quite a few cases that were dropped at the preliminary stage. And as for dragging people into the studio, we don't put a rope around their necks. Mr. Koda obtains their full consent. Otherwise they'd never stay sitting in front of the cameras, would they?"

"And do they also consent to having a camera crew raid their bedrooms?"

"No, that's—" Kiyokawa pursed his lips and broke off, then went on uncertainly. "I don't think we'd be using the footage unless they'd given their consent afterward."

"So according to you, she—or he as the case may be—is just thrilled to pieces about having the film shown and going before the cameras?"

"No," Kiyokawa burst out impatiently, "you know that's not what I'm saying. Of course most people don't like it. What I meant was that they change their minds when they talk to Mr. Koda. He persuades them to appear. And anyway, why should an adult man or woman disappear without a word? How can they expect to get away with it?"

"So he goes about it by threatening and coaxing. He tells them 'You owe it to yourself to appear, to present your side of the story, if you don't want to be thought an inhuman brute.' These are amateurs he's dealing with. With the authority of the TV station behind him he can get almost anyone to do what he says. Is that really any different from dragging them in against their will on the end of a rope?"

Finding himself at a loss for words, Kiyokawa scratched his head. "I give up! That's not what I was getting at—"

"Whatever you were getting at, it all comes down to the same thing: invasion of privacy, an assault backed by the authority of the media. Listen, Dai." Nakazawa leaned forward. Thrusting his glowing triangular face close to Kiyokawa's, he propped his elbows on his spread knees and held out his open palms as if to demonstrate his point.

"Is it a crime to go missing? Hell, no. It might be grounds for divorce but there's no law against a married woman going into hiding with another man. No matter how unfaithful a husband and wife are to each other, as long as it doesn't develop into a criminal case the law doesn't become involved. Why not? Because it's a matter of personal morality. There's no reason for the state to interfere. And there's no reason for anybody else to interfere, either." Nakazawa waved his open hands emphatically. "Even the state hasn't wanted to enforce what Koda is enforcing in that program. You say he carries out a careful investigation before he chooses his subjects? What's the basis for his choice, then? It's Koda. Koda's own morals. Koda decides that this wife or that husband ought to be hauled in to defend themselves on TV, and he goes ahead and does it. Koda messes with other people's lives according to his own morality. And that's not all. If their motives for doing the searches were as altruistic as you say, why would they put them on TV? Why would they shoot those ugly scenes and show them? It's obvious, isn't it? He's making an example of them. He's passing judgment on these missing people according to his own code. Besides"—Nakazawa raised the index finger of one hand—"it's good show business. He knows he can increase the ratings if he makes these judgmental programs of his shocking enough. And he doesn't care whose privacy he tramples on to do it."

Kiyokawa's broad shoulders were slumped. He didn't say a word.

"Neither Koda nor the studio has any right to do that." Nakazawa picked up his glass and leaned back. Kiyokawa folded his arms, heaved a sigh, and twisted his stiff neck two or three times.

"Drink up, Dai. Something wrong?"

Nodding silently, Kiyokawa helped himself to ice and a refill. Nakazawa's technician commented, "Lately, I'm told, they're using all sorts of tricks to liven up the show."

"So I've heard," said Nakazawa.

"On the current one, the rumor is that he deliberately set them up to run off again. Do you think he can be trusted? Won't the press get onto him sooner or later?"

"Let's not talk about it anymore. It's too depressing for our innocent young friend Daisuke." Nakazawa laughed happily. "Come on, Dai. It goes with the territory. No need to get depressed. You just have to realize things aren't as simple as they look. It could do you a lot of good to work on a top show like that. So as long as you're there, why not think of ways to restrain Maestro Koda a little?"

Nakazawa's eyes came to rest on the door behind Kiyokawa's back. His happy expression quickly faded and he muttered to his companion, "Like to go somewhere else?"

"Sure, let's get out of here."

"You staying, Dai?"

"Yes."

"I'll leave you my bottle, then."

The two men got up and headed for the door, the owner and the girl bidding them farewell as they passed. Tendo, who had just sat down at the bar, turned.

"Oh, hello there." Nakazawa sounded as if he'd only just spotted him.

"Well, well," Tendo replied.

Nakazawa smiled with the corners of his mouth. "This is a surprise. The great Tendo doesn't often grace such a humble establishment with his presence."

"Now, now," Tendo said good-humoredly. "I was over at the Mitaya. Hadn't been there for the longest time. And I remembered I'd been forgetting to show my face around here, too. Oh, by the way, you did an excellent job on that talk show—the one on the obscenity trial."

Nakazawa shrugged. "The ratings were bad."

"You mustn't worry about the ratings. Not worrying about the ratings is your strong point. It's the key to making quality programs."

"I wish I could believe you meant that." Nakazawa gave another shrug, then suddenly turned formal. "Well, if you'll excuse us . . ."

He went out with the technician. Kiyokawa stood at Tendo's elbow. "Good evening."

"Oh, Dai, I didn't know you were here, too."

"I wonder if it would be possible for me to get a transfer?"

"What's this? I don't like drunks."

"I'm not drunk." The words were a little slurred. "I'm worn out from working on that show." Kiyokawa rubbed the side of his face.

After studying him for a moment, Tendo said, "Right. Let's sit over there," and led the way to the back table. While they waited for the girl to finish rearranging it, Tendo asked, "What's wrong?"

Kiyokawa managed to overcome his hesitation. "I don't like being assigned to Mr. Koda."

"Have you had a fight?"

Kiyokawa shook his head like a little boy. Tendo started to laugh. "You've been talking to Nakazawa, haven't you?"

Kiyokawa was silent.

"What did he say? Out with it."

After a swallow of whisky Kiyokawa answered. "That Mr. Koda makes those programs to punish people according to his own moral judgments. And he makes them shocking to get good ratings. It's an invasion of privacy and the studio is committing a crime."

"That's what I expected him to say."

Warming his brandy glass in both hands, Tendo went on, "Don't let it bother you. The Tuesday ratings are so outstanding, I'm sure they make the other programs suffer by comparison. There isn't a single director who has a good word to say about Koda. Nakazawa's in a particularly bad slump and his bosses are always threatening him with cancellation."

"It's not just what he said. I've been trying all along not to let it get to me, but I know that there's a lot of truth in what he said. Especially in this latest case."

"Oh?" Interest flickered in Tendo's eyes.

"It was when we went to film the apartment where Mrs. Yamashita and Kakimoto were—well, hiding. It was the first time I'd gone out with one of those crews, you see. When we went in, Mr. Yamashita got excited and attacked his wife with his fists. I grabbed his arm to hold him back. And then Mr. Koda pulled me away by the shoulder. He was going like this—" Kiyokawa gave a vigorous shake of his head. "I was so surprised, I dropped Mr. Yamashita's arm. Of course he went for his wife instantly, punching and kicking and dragging her—it was terrible to watch. I went to stop him again and again, but Mr. Koda was holding me back by the shoulder the whole time. He wouldn't let me do it. Then after he'd watched Mr. Yamashita on the rampage for long enough, he called out 'Now, now' or something like that and signaled me to step in. And we finally stopped them. It was disgusting."

Glowering, Kiyokawa raised his whisky glass. Tendo asked calmly, "What else happened?"

Kiyokawa glared up at him. "You know the background to the second disappearance, don't you? How Kakimoto came to find out what hospital Mrs. Yamashita was in?"

"You accidentally gave it away, right?"

"Right. That's what happened. So perhaps it'll only sound like I'm making excuses, but—that day Kakimoto had come to see Mr. Koda about something. They were talking in the reception room. Then Mr. Koda came out and said to me, 'How about taking Mr. Kakimoto out for a drink? He's very depressed.' I thought 'Oh hell,' but I reminded myself that it was all in the day's work and I invited Kakimoto out. As we were leaving, Mr. Koda called me over and warned me to keep quiet about the hospital. But he put it like this: I don't want you to tell Kakimoto. That might prove difficult, how-ever, as he's sure to be fishing for information. And one can understand his wanting to see her one last time. That was the tone of what he said. When you think about it, yes, he was hushing me up, but he gave me the impression that maybe he wouldn't object if I were to tell. . . .''

"I know what you mean." Tendo's shoulders quivered with laughter.

"You know? When he put it like that and Kakimoto broke down and cried, I gave the address away. Of course it was careless of me. I reported back to Mr. Koda and got my knuckles rapped. 'After I'd expressly warned you to keep it quiet,' he said. That was when I thought, 'Hold on a minute, something's funny here.' Now I'm convinced that Mr. Koda used me. And on top of that I heard later at the hospital that Mr. Koda had been seen in the vicinity that night. And again the next morning—the day they went missing."

"Is that so?"

"It looks like he was waiting to see them go, doesn't it? Though it's hard to believe."

"I see. Yes, I can see it would make you suspicious."

Tendo seemed to be enjoying himself. Kiyokawa tossed an ice cube into his mouth and crunched it. "What do you think?" he asked.

"About what?"

"Is Mr. Koda doing the show to punish people? And for the ratings?"

"Who knows?" Tendo said airily, "I'm not a mind reader. All I know is that Koda's program gets the ratings. And the whole station depends on it. Thanks to that program, a bunch of directors who don't have a good word to say for Koda can keep their own hands clean and still keep their jobs. Seems to me that anybody who earns his living at the station has no cause to hate Koda. They should all be grateful. Dai, I'd go so far as to say that it's Koda who's paying your salary."

"I don't *hate* Mr. Koda," Kiyokawa said hastily. "But if he's invading people's privacy, I think there's a problem. For one thing, it makes me an accomplice."

"Privacy. Hmm." Tendo studied Kiyokawa's grim face before asking, "What do you make of the people who apply for the searches? And what about the missing persons?"

"What do you mean?"

"What do you think of people like the Yamashitas and Kakimoto? Do you respect them?"

"No, not at all. They're all a bit peculiar. If I were in their shoes—either way—I'd never want to display my private life on TV like that. I don't know if they're stupid, or ignorant, or— "

"That's it. They're stupid and ignorant."

Tendo said this so flatly that Kiyokawa was stunned. Fixing him with clear eyes, Tendo went on. "Why do you think the ratings are so high?"

"Oh, because—a lot of people watch."

"That's right. The public loves it. That sordid show."

Kiyokawa was stunned again.

"When I say sordid, I'm speaking in terms of my own personal tastes. I would never be so arrogant as to force those tastes on the viewers. Television doesn't belong to me, it belongs to the public, and it must be responsive to public demand. As the makers of what goes on television, it's our job to deliver what the public wants. One way or another. It can't be helped if in the process the privacy of stupid and ignorant people has to be sacrificed to some extent. What does that matter if you look at the valuable services that television as a whole is providing?"

"I guess you're right, if you look at it as a whole." Kiyokawa grew pensive. He looked up again to ask: "But what about the press? Won't we come under attack if we go too far?"

Tendo suppressed a smile. "Even on the papers that belong to our company's group, how many journalists do you imagine are aware of that program's existence? As luck would have it, the more a journalist cares about human rights the less likely he is ever to watch the women's programs. You can bet he thoroughly despises them. Anyway, if they were so sensitive about the right to privacy there'd have been an outcry ten years back when TV first started searching for runaways. It was quieter then—the anchorman simply showed a photograph and gave a description and asked viewers to cooperate. The outcome was announced in a later program. But the rights of the runaways who were put on TV's wanted list were being invaded just as blatantly then as they are now. I thought to myself back then that TV had started trespassing on people's privacy. But not one voice was raised in protest. If the press was too insensitive to react then, you can be sure it won't react now. And on top of everything else, have you any idea how pathetic the ratings are when a program treats a human-rights issue seriously?"

Flashing a smile, Tendo concluded, "The public aren't interested in other people's rights. Except while they're enjoying the sight of them being violated."

THE HOST

Having surprised Akari by declaring that Koda made him sick, Hidaka moved to their table with its plain white floral-patterned cloth, opened the large leather-bound menu with a gesture of greater anticipation than he ever showed in opening a book, and deliberated over his choice.

First, for Akari: a half-dozen oysters on ice, mushroom salad, sea-urchin potage, and duck with pepper sauce. For himself: melon and prosciutto, palmitos salad, sea-urchin potage, and roast lamb with mint sauce. To complete the order he asked the wine steward for a dry wine. "I'll leave it to you. Just don't bankrupt me," he begged, making the waiter laugh. Then he added a further request, this time to Akari: no discussing the job during their meal.

Hidaka chose his subject to suit the lights of the city spread below, the candlelight, and the bouquet of the wine. Men and women, in other words. He advanced a number of general ideas which Akari tackled as heartily as the food. If the going seemed to be getting too heavy, Hidaka would unerringly lighten it with a joke. And from time to time he illustrated his theories with the example of Akari and himself.

As the meal progressed and the wine bottle emptied, the cloak of generalization fell easily away.

This was the essence of Hidaka's argument: You're too doctrinaire about love. It's the repressive education given to middle-class girls that does it. You're practicing a sort of mortification of the flesh, Christian-style. If you were liberated in spirit—like me, and the women I know—you could enjoy sex for its own sake and you'd realize there's no reason for all this denial. Look, compared to your so-called "true love," the games I play cause no one any pain. It's only an unenlightened girlish romanticism that makes you reject what I'm saying.

Of course I'm not mortifying my flesh, Akari argued in return, nor am I negative about sex. And that's why I don't like the idea of turning it into a game. It seems to me that the games you play are an escape from what you call "true love." Maybe true love is often painful, but wouldn't the enlightened and courageous thing be to try and work out how not to hurt each other? I've no objection to other people enjoying a game, but I'm not so sure they *are* actually enjoying it. I wonder whether your girlfriends and your wife are completely happy with the relationships you have?

Whenever they drew too close to his own personal affairs, Hidaka took refuge in a defiant lack of seriousness or a fine unconcern for what others thought. This kept them from clashing and preserved a certain mood that went with the night and the candlelight and the wine.

By the time their dessert of crêpes and orange sauce was prepared on a wagon by the table, the wine bottle stood empty. Hidaka had emptied it while Akari's first glass stayed unfinished. Hidaka was lively and talkative. Over coffee, Akari conscientiously brought up the subject of the job again. Hidaka said in disgust:

"Young lady, do you think I like doing that program? Do I look stupid? Don't go lumping me with Shichiro Ogu and Kojiro Sasaki. You're absolutely right: that program is unbearable. It's up to the individuals concerned whether they stay together or break up or run out on each other. What business is it of TV's? Now, if it were the deserted husband who gave us an earful of his problems it might make some sense, but it's Koda and all those smug panelists holding forth and telling people what to do. Who the hell do they think they are? It'd be a different matter if they meant to stick with the couple for the rest of their lives. But they mean to do nothing of the sort. It's a job to Koda, to Sasaki, to the lot of them. They sit on their backsides and pontificate. It's insufferable. Koda has absolutely no right to preach morality to runaways—if you think about what he does himself on that program."

"You mean those terrible videos. I think they're cruel."

"Not only that. You probably don't know about all his dirty dealings."

"What dirty dealings?"

"For example, before they ever do the appeal they've located the missing person themselves. That kind of thing."

"Is that right?" Akari's eyes widened.

"Yes, indeed. I don't want to be involved any more than I have to, so I'm careful to avoid hearing the details, but I expect that's not all he does either, not by a long shot."

"That's terrible," Akari muttered.

"Even if it weren't for that, I wouldn't like what he's doing. He turns the public into informers. And who are these people they're tracking down? Runaways. Not murderers. On top of abusing the rights of the missing persons, he encourages the viewers to think like stool pigeons. What gets me is that Koda himself is totally unaware of the implications of what he's doing. Most likely he sincerely believes he's making a fine upstanding program for the good of society, a program that strikes a blow for justice. Of all fools, that's the kind of fool I detest the most."

"It's true, they do abuse people's rights and they do encourage the public to turn them in, don't they?"

Hidaka cast a glance at the night lights of the city below. "And then of course there are the fools who love to watch the show. But TV ought to be ethical. We know that popular support doesn't necessarily make a thing right—look at Imperial Japan, or Hitler. We oughtn't to be pandering to mass tastes. The makers of the programs, the people who stoke up that proto-Fascist machinery, ought to have a firm ethical basis for what they do, even at the risk sometimes of losing their public. Otherwise there'll be trouble. Or rather, there is trouble already."

"Can't something be done about the program?" Akari said, giving Hidaka a very earnest gaze.

The fight quickly went out of his eyes; instead he smiled amiably. "I'm only a poor struggling personality."

"Nonsense. All the directors respect your opinion. You're included in the planning for the other days of the week, aren't you?"

"No, not for *Showbiz Report* on Fridays."

"Yes, but you're in charge of planning *Stories from the Crime File* on Mondays and *People In Depth* on Wednesdays, aren't you? If there's anyone who can get Mr. Koda and Mr. Tendo to change the program, it's you."

"You overestimate me."

"How can you know unless you try?"

"All I can do is keep my own involvement to a minimum. I've flatly refused to take part in discussions with the panel or help with the appeals. After that it's Koda's and Tendo's territory. I know nothing."

Hidaka shrugged wearily. Akari wouldn't let it go at that. "But that doesn't affect the program itself."

"No."

Akari was at a loss for words. She turned away with a look of extreme dissatisfaction. "I wonder if I should say something to Mr. Koda?" she asked, and bit her lip.

"You do what you like." Hidaka was watching Akari with a gleam in his eyes.

Glancing quickly at him, she said, "Look, I just can't stand the thought of being part of something like that. Though if *I* go to them, I'll probably only get myself fired."

"The same goes for me." Hidaka sighed. "It's all very well for you. For you it's easy come, easy go." After a long look at Akari's dubious expression, he frowned and continued. "For you the job is two years of fun. Whether you work out your contract or quit in the middle, either way you won't be staying in TV. You can make your escape from an ugly program, and no doubt you'll get married and have kids and your conscience will be clear. While television and society will go on precisely as before. It's easy enough for you to talk."

Akari looked startled.

"I can't do that," he continued. "I can't take the risk of complaining about a program with amazing ratings and finding myself out of a job. It's not only my livelihood that's at stake. I'm in this for the leverage it gives me. You'll admit that on the other days' programs and in the magazine pieces I write and so on, I try to do a worthwhile job?"

Akari nodded in silence.

"When you try to do a worthwhile job you meet with resistance. You need leverage. A lot of that leverage comes from fame. In other words, there are times when being the host of *Good Afternoon, Ladies* enables me to overcome the resistance and do a good job elsewhere. If I were dropped it would become that much more difficult to do the work I'm doing elsewhere. And the really frightening thing is that whoever they brought in to replace me would most certainly be worse. As long as I'm there, at least the other days of the week are safe. But just you let someone else try: every show would toe the line, they'd go all out for the ratings any way they could. If you only knew how hard I have to fight even now. . . ."

"Yes, it must be hard."

"TV's rotten, it's hopelessly corrupt. To tell you the truth, I'd get out like a shot if I could. But right now I need the foothold. I don't like what I'm doing." Nodding as if to say "I rest my case," Hidaka let his strained face relax. Akari was deep in thought.

After a while she said, "So what it comes down to is this: as long as the program has top ratings, nothing can be done?"

"That's right."

Hidaka stretched and said laughingly, "The comedy shows and late-night shows I used to work on in the old days—which were wildly popular—were the first to be attacked by the associations for protection of community standards. But the old ladies don't seem to mind Koda's show at all." Then he put his face closer to Akari's. "You really are beautiful when you have that thoughtful look. Excuse me a moment," and he left the table. Akari, her chin resting on her hand, went on gazing ahead into space. Confusion, indignation, helplessness came and went across her features. Fully ten minutes later, she suddenly looked around for Hidaka. He was nowhere to be seen. Akari's gaze traveled anxiously back and forth to the dark gap of the exit, to the piano lounge where showers of glass droplets hung and glittered from the ceiling, to the other tables and the diners' faces in a warm red glow of candlelight, and finally returned to her own table where it fell on a single red rose bud lying beneath the candle.

"Oh," she said out loud. The last time she'd looked, the rose had been in the slender vase beside the candle. Just as she put out her hand she noticed a slip of white paper under the stem. She picked it up. On it, written in English in slanting handwriting, was *"8th floor. 812. I'm waiting for you."*

She closed her hand quickly over the paper and looked around in astonishment, blinking rapidly. Then, setting her mouth firmly and taking a deep breath, she squared her shoulders and left the restaurant. All the way down in the elevator and along the eighth-floor corridor to the door marked *812*, Akari had a purposeful look, and she was still resolute as she knocked on the door. It opened and there was Hidaka in a terry-cloth dressing gown.

"Mr. Hidaka, I—"

"Shh. No yelling in the corridor. Quick, quick."

Hidaka whispered as gleefully as a mischievous child, stepping back as he motioned Akari inside. Akari's poise seemed to desert her as she stepped into the room. Hidaka took her arm and drew her closer with one hand while he closed the door with the other.

"Mr. Hidaka, I—" Hidaka's lips stopped her. After a second Akari began to struggle furiously.

"Ow!" Hidaka let go and grabbed his shin, screwing up his face and just managing not to shout with pain. Then he limped to the bed, still yelping, and fell faceup across it.

From the doorway Akari said, "I came to tell you I'm going home. I didn't really mean to kick you."

"Damn it."

"I'm sorry." Akari apologized with a worried look.

"No problem. I'm all right. Ow!"

Though his face was still twisted, Hidaka was chuckling to himself. After a moment's bewilderment Akari put a hand to her head and brushed back her hair, then said quietly, "Good-bye. Thanks for the dinner," turned smartly, and left. She strode away down the corridor, but after passing countless identical doors without arriving at the elevators, she discovered she was walking in the wrong direction. "Oh for goodness' sake." She wheeled about and tiptoed in spite of herself as she passed Hidaka's room. As she did so she overheard his voice inside. She stopped short.

"Ah, so you're in. . . . Can you come over right away? . . . Yes, I am. . . . An *hour*? That's an awfully long time. . . . Who cares what you're wearing? You'll only be taking it off anyway. . . . Okay, forty minutes. I can't wait any longer. . . . Yes, come straight up. Eight-one-two. Got that? Eight-one-two."

With a start Akari caught herself eavesdropping and broke into a run toward the elevators.

STANDING BY

The lines that had been scanning ceaselessly for over nineteen hours—since shortly after six on Monday morning—finally stopped just after midnight Tuesday and took a five-hour break.

Nobuo Koda slept three hours longer. Even so, he was at the studio bright and early while most of those who sent out *Good Afternoon, Ladies* nationwide were still sound asleep. Every Tuesday he would reach his desk between 7:30 and 8:00 and double-check every detail. If Kiyokawa failed to appear by 8:30 he would promptly phone his home in case he'd overslept.

There was no need to phone this morning: Daisuke Kiyokawa arrived shortly before the half hour. But after one look at his bloated face, Koda warned him—to his intense embarrassment—not to overindulge the night before the program. About the time Koda finished his briefing, the floor director, cameramen, and lighting and sound crews reported for work. At 9:00, they assembled in the briefing room, scripts were distributed, and the technical directions—the order of items, changes in the camera work, et cetera—were finalized. When that was done the crew dispersed to their positions and prepared to go on air.

Kiyokawa went over to the Mitaya to fetch Fukuko. He didn't think she looked as haggard this morning with her hair nicely washed. When the proprietress followed him out to ask quietly,

"What shall I do about the room?" Kiyokawa thought awhile and replied, "Please wait till you hear from Mr. Koda." He then escorted Fukuko to the special waiting room on the second floor and kept her company for ten minutes or so before leaving her with the part-timer who attended to guests. Downstairs again he checked on the other arrivals and the progress of preparations.

In the tearoom that had just opened in the lobby, Shichiro Ogu, Kojiro Sasaki (who'd been asked to come in early), and Koda were meanwhile drinking coffee and making a final check.

"That Kakimoto's got a nerve." Sasaki traded on his reputation for eloquent plain-speaking, and now he spoke through his thick lips with frank disgust. His upper lip curled back till it almost touched the tip of his long nose. A pink handkerchief screamed from the breast pocket of his jacket, which had a broad diagonal navy-and-white check and was worn over a pink shirt and a white tie with a large picture of a tiger lily on it.

"What the hell's he playing at? After he swore black and blue he'd break up with her. You agree with me, don't you, Ogu? And after I'd listened to his troubles for hours and even fed him dinner."

Grinning, Ogu said, "I'll bet you passed it on to us."

"Of course. I've got to charge for expenses at least. I'm not in this for the fun of it. Can't expect me to put up with people's boring affairs for nothing. But that's not the point. You know what I mean, Mr. Koda? It's a question of feelings—ours."

Koda nodded deeply in agreement.

"I'd like to smash his face in. That's how I feel. It's a crying shame he isn't coming today," Sasaki spluttered indignantly.

Koda said, "So today I'd like Mr. Sasaki to express his views in this regard perfectly plainly. Since our viewers feel just as strongly, he will be expressing their point of view."

"Fine. Leave it to me. I'll tell it to them straight. I won't pull any punches," Sasaki promised darkly.

Once Koda had left them, he leaned over to Ogu. "Know what I think? To make Fukuko Yamashita go off her head like that, Kakimoto must've had a big dick."

"I'll bet her old man wasn't up to it."

"Could be. Or could be Fukuko's a good lay. A woman like that, you don't give her a second glance, but they can be hot for it. She's built like this, right?" Sasaki solemnly drew curves in the air. "She's a hot one, you can tell. She's the type who goes out of her mind. Froths at the mouth. Passes out."

Ogu nudged Sasaki and gave him a knowing sidelong look. "Is it true, Sasaki—did you do it with the last wife from the show?"

"What?"

"You know—the one with the huge false eyelashes. The kind of weird one."

"Oh, the one before last. Give me a break. I have got *some* taste. That was Hayami. Yes, it was Kimio Hayami who had her, or so I heard."

"Are you sure?"

"Wasn't it?"

"The way I heard it, it was you."

"Get outta here."

Koda had gone from the tearoom to the special waiting room on the second floor where he welcomed Fukuko. She was sitting across from the part-timer at a loss for conversation. Koda spoke encouragingly about how she should approach the discussion. Fukuko reported that she had decided to ask for a divorce.

"I've begun to think that maybe I can be strong," she said.

Koda, however, preferred not to deal in such specifics if he could avoid it.

Close to 10:30, black limousines pulled up outside one by one, each flying the company's pennant, and the lobby began to fill up. From the half-hour on, all the participants except Kazushi Hidaka gathered as usual in the tearoom.

Across from Ogu and Sasaki, Akari Kasai sat with the writer Hiroshi Fujiwara. Fujiwara, in a plain tweed jacket, black shirt, and tan scarf, had greasy graying hair that straggled at the sides of his face; he always hunched his shoulders and had a cigarette in his mouth. He looked far older than his actual age of fifty-two or fifty-three, perhaps because it had taken him longer than usual to make his name in the literary world. He was often to be seen on television giving personal advice or taking part in debates. Nobody was sure why Fujiwara, with his grave and ponderous manner, made such casual appearances—whether for fun, or fame, or fortune—but whatever the reason he was undoubtedly valuable to the *Looking for Love* series, which tended to be short on figures who could lend an air of authority.

Sitting with her back to Fujiwara was another writer, Kikuko Morisaki. This sixtyish woman, dressed in a grayish-lilac wool dress with her long hair gathered in a bun, had joined the panel through Fujiwara's introduction; unlike him, however, she appeared only on this program. She was an altogether unspectacular writer, and though most of the people who watched the program might have been aware that she was a novelist, they could not have named any of her novels.

Next to Morisaki was Kimio Hayami, continuity director, pop show host, reporter on late-night adult programs, and occasional debater. He sat, looking pleasant enough, but barely able to stay awake, his spreading middle-aged body clad in the kind of tailored suit an elite company man might wear.

Across from him, Kay Arlemois, owner of a dozen beauty salons, wore the lustrous smile that never left her face while anybody was watching. She was dressed in evening wear: a long dress made up of yards of bright red organdy, its low neck and gathered sleeves embroidered in gold. Her nails were red, her face many-hued, her hair dyed a reddish brown; pink foundation cream had been applied from her bosom (on which hung a string of pearls) to her shoulders, leaving no outlet anywhere for her age. Trapped inside, it gave her a certain lurid quality.

Next to her the lawyer Setsuko Noto seemed a very ordinary type. If she hadn't been beside Kay Arlemois, this middle-aged woman in a mannish suit of saffron yellow, with the whites of her eyes rather prominent and the corners of her mouth downturned, would have qualified as distinctive enough herself.

Sitting alone at the neighboring table and engrossed in looking something up was a lawyer colleague of Noto's, Takashi Kawamura. At thirty-seven or thirty-eight he appeared to be every inch the well-dressed, well-mannered, white-collar worker. Neither Noto nor Kawamura was especially articulate or interesting as a personality and neither had ever been invited onto other channels or shows. They featured exclusively in this series, where they added a touch of legal authority to the panel.

Thus, drinking coffee, chatting to their nearest neighbors, smoking, not talking, and looking things up, these nine passed the time till they were called to the studio.

About 11:00, Takao Yamashita entered the building and was shown to a waiting room close to the first-floor studio. Koda was informed and went to greet him, followed by Ogu and Sasaki, who were summoned from the tearoom. Yamashita was dead set against a divorce. Sasaki discussed his plans excitedly, offering alternatives and advice on how best to present himself.

"I'm counting on you especially, Sasaki Sensei," Yamashita told him.

At about the same time, Akari went into the studio for a camera rehearsal of the live commercial spot. Kiyokawa relayed directions from the control room and the floor director gave clearly visible cues. In the meantime Koda entered the control room and took the director's seat. When the camera rehearsal was over, Akari made her way to the first-floor waiting room. The two lawyers and Hayami were there with Ogu and Sasaki, keeping Yamashita company. Once she had welcomed the guest, Akari withdrew quietly to a corner.

At 11:40, the floor director came for them on the run. They all trooped into the studio: Fujiwara, Morisaki, and Kay Arlemois from the tearoom; Yamashita, Ogu, Akari, Sasaki, Hayami, Noto, and Kawamura from the first-floor waiting room.

Koda and Kiyokawa came down to greet them in the studio, then the floor director seated each as predetermined. At this stage Kazushi Hidaka came into the building and walked directly into the studio. Hidaka never arrived any sooner than this on a Tuesday. He said a cheerful hello to Koda, to Kiyokawa, to the crew and the panel, and chatted with each member. When he caught sight of Akari, he limped a step or two.

Takao Yamashita was seated in the center of the large round-table set. To his right the lineup was Kojiro Sasaki, Hiroshi Fujiwara, Kikuko Morisaki, Kimio Hayami, Setsuko Noto, Takashi Kawamura, and Kay Arlemois. A place was reserved between Morisaki and Hayami for Fukuko, who would be brought into the studio later on. There was enough space for the cameras to circle the table freely for front shots of each.

Away to the right of this set was another, a desk with a floral decoration against a large background panel across the top of which was the *Good Afternoon, Ladies* logo. Seated in the middle here was Kazushi Hidaka, on his left Akari Kasai, and on his right Shichiro Ogu. All three faced out into the dimly lit studio area toward the closed double doors on its far side. Within that area, cameras and people circulated.

Koda and Kiyokawa returned to the control room. All was ready at last. There was no visible sign of tension in the studio. A buzz of private conversations continued beneath the louder voices calling across the room.

"Three minutes," the floor director announced. Everyone in the outwardly unchanging studio was gradually coming under a control focused in one direction. Everyone noted the time. They glanced now and then at the wall clock or a wristwatch, ran through their duties, and rehearsed what they had to do.

"One minute. Stand by for the commercial break." Private conversations ceased or dropped to a whisper. The people under the lights cleared their throats and checked their appearance.

Into the soundless studio came a bouncy jingle as a picture flashed onto the monitor.

"First commercial. One minute," the floor director announced matter-of-factly.

ON THE AIR

The show's theme, a sprightly number by a female chorus, is heard. The cameras, which have been pointing this way and that, focus on the three figures at the table. The three break off their conversation and straighten up as if suddenly aware of the cameras.

HIDAKA: Today's another very lovely day.

AKARI: I expect our viewers at home have their hands full with the washing.

OGU: But I hope you'll take a break and join us—it's time for *Good Afternoon, Ladies.*

HIDAKA: I'm your host, Kazushi Hidaka.

OGU: Your co-hosts, the irrepressible Shichiro Ogu—

AKARI: And Akari Kasai.

OGU: You know, Mr. Hidaka, we've been hearing a lot lately about police inquiries that seem to implicate a number of show-business personalities in a baseball gambling syndicate with underworld connections. . . .

HIDAKA: I hope you're clean?

OGU: Who, me? (*He laughs.*) I'm clean. But it's a nasty business, isn't it?

HIDAKA: It certainly is. We'll be taking a closer look on Friday in our *Showbiz Report*. But today we have another installment in our series *Looking for Love*.

AKARI: And as usual we have our panel of counselors with us in the studio.

OGU: In fact, we're going to be following developments in the story of Mr. and Mrs. Yamashita, whose case we've been covering on the program for some time now. You'll remember Mrs. Yamashita had disappeared for a second time? Well, she's been found.

HIDAKA: Has she now?

OGU: She has, and we've asked Mr. and Mrs. Yamashita into the studio to talk things over and, we hope, really sort out their marital problems this time.

HIDAKA: Hmm. It does seem a difficult situation, but let's hope we can arrive at a happy ending.

OGU: We'll be joining the Yamashitas in just a moment.

HIDAKA: Right after these messages.

The three hosts bow; a commercial break follows. The sound is cut off in the studio; only the picture comes up on the monitor while they prepare for the next segment. The three hosts at the desk reappear on the screen.

HIDAKA: Now back to *Looking for Love* and the Yamashitas. Before we have Mr. and Mrs. Yamashita join us, we should quickly remind the audience at home of the situation so far.

OGU: I'll run over the main developments. (*Using a pointer, he indicates the items on a panel that Akari is holding.*) First, on the fourteenth of last month Mrs. Fukuko Yamashita, the wife of bicycle shop owner Mr. Takao Yamashita, suddenly disappeared, leaving him with their three children. The shop's assistant, Mr. Eiji Kakimoto, disappeared at the same time. (*Kakimoto's photograph, name, and age are shown on another camera.*) Having searched everywhere, in desperation Mr. Yamashita appealed to his wife on this program.

HIDAKA: (*Looking at the script:*) That was on November sixth, wasn't it?

OGU: Yes. And Mrs. Yamashita was in fact located at that time, as we'll see.

The videotape of Yamashita walking down the apartment corridor starts. All eyes in the studio turn to the monitor. Reactions vary: some watch open-mouthed, some quickly lower their eyes, some laugh to themselves, some frown. The video ends.

OGU: Fukuko was located, but when the Yamashitas and Mr. Kakimoto were unable to reach a settlement, Mr. Yamashita asked us for the expert help of our panel. Mrs. Yamashita and Mr. Kakimoto agreed to come into the studio and on the thirteenth their problems were discussed on this program.

HIDAKA: And as a result Mrs. Yamashita agreed to return home. Would that be correct?

OGU: Up to a point. But let's take another look.

The video of Yamashita and Fukuko seated opposite each other begins. Everyone watches as Yamashita demands that Fukuko have an abortion and Fukuko consents in tears.

OGU: You see, Fukuko was pregnant with Mr. Kakimoto's child. The film you've just seen was made immediately after our program ended on the thirteenth. As you saw, Mrs. Yamashita made up her mind to part from Mr. Kakimoto. She entered a hospital and had the operation.

HIDAKA: She then disappeared again, this time from the hospital, with Mr. Kakimoto.

OGU: Yes, indeed she did. Taking us completely by surprise.

HIDAKA: And on last week's program Mr. Yamashita made a second appeal.

OGU: Yes. And it was at that point that we left the story last week.

HIDAKA: Where did the runaways go?

OGU: (*Heavily:*) To Kagoshima.

HIDAKA: As far as that?

OGU: Yes. It seems they were ready to die together. Fortunately, thanks to information provided by a viewer, we were able to trace their whereabouts.

HIDAKA: That *was* fortunate. Suicide wouldn't have solved anything.

AKARI: They must have been desperately unhappy.

OGU: But, Akari, think of the husband she'd deserted. Think of the children. What good would it have done to kill herself? She is an adult, even if she can't behave like one.

HIDAKA: Now, let's not fight among ourselves.

OGU: Oh, sorry, I was carried away.

HIDAKA: So today we have Mrs. Yamashita here with us?

OGU: We do.

HIDAKA: And Eiji Kakimoto?

OGU: I'm glad you asked me that. There's been a setback where he's concerned. We'll have more details after the break.

HIDAKA: But first, this message.

Akari has already slipped from her seat and circled behind the cameras to take her place on the set for the live commercial. With a bright smile she picks up the product and speaks her lines from memory. The young man from the advertising agency watches intently beside the camera. In the meantime the door opens quietly on the far side of the dimly lit studio and Fukuko comes in with the part-timer and Kiyokawa. The door closes, Kiyokawa remaining

outside to return to the control room. The floor director seats
Fukuko, who keeps her eyes downcast. Yamashita watches her like
a hawk. The commercial ends with a close-up of the product. The
camera returns to Hidaka's head and shoulders at the desk.

HIDAKA: We have with us our panel of counselors. (*He watches the*
monitor as the cameras cut to the panelists one by one, while
titles give their names and professions.) First, as usual we have
the authors Mr. Hiroshi Fujiwara and Mrs. Kikuko Morisaki,
our old friend Mr. Kojiro Sasaki, and Mr. Kimio Hayami. Next
to him is the lawyer Mrs. Setsuko Noto, and Mr. Takashi
Kawamura, also a lawyer. And today it's my pleasure to welcome to our panel Mrs. Kay Arlemois, a beautician with a
wealth of life experience. (*He turns to the front camera as its*
red light comes on again.) Well, shall we begin? Over to you,
Mr. Ogu.

OGU: (*Standing between Sasaki and Fujiwara with a microphone in*
his hand:) Fine. (*He surveys the panelists.*) Actually, before we
get started I have an admission to make: Mr. Eiji Kakimoto—
the man who twice ran off with Mrs. Yamashita—is not in the
studio today.

SASAKI: What! Why not?

OGU: He's gone home.

SASAKI: How come? (*He leans back to look up at Ogu.*) Does this
mean he's broken off with Mrs. Yamashita?

OGU: I suppose it does. Doesn't it, Mrs. Yamashita?

FUKUKO: (*The camera moves in, but she doesn't reply.*)

SASAKI: Is that right? Well, is it?

FUKUKO: (*In a small voice:*) Yes.

SASAKI: I don't believe this. I mean, didn't I just hear somebody say
that you went to Kagoshima to die together? After breaking the
promises you made right here in front of everybody. What
does he mean by simply clearing out now?

OGU: We did tell him we'd like him at least to come on to the program and explain whatever he'd decided to do, in view of all the trouble the panel had gone to and our viewers' concern for him. But he refused to do so.

SASAKI: (*Striking the table:*) Hah! Then he's run out on us, that's what he's done. Hasn't he?

HAYAMI: Well, I don't know if I'd put it quite like that. He's free to do what he wants to.

SASAKI: No, I can't accept that, Hayami. He had a duty to come, if you ask me. Look, the two of them (*pointing to Fukuko*) started all this, right? It's not *our* problem. And here we are out of the goodness of our hearts getting together and trying to give them the best advice we can. I've spent a lot of time with that Kakimoto, listening to him go on about—

OGU: We have the video here of Mr. Kakimoto declaring his intention to end the relationship. Let's take a look, shall we?

The video of Kakimoto in tears is screened. Sasaki nods at his own comments on the tape. The video ends.

SASAKI: Remember that took place after we'd gone off the air, outside the studio. And even after that I felt so sorry for him that I took him out for a meal and gave him all kinds of tips for his future. And then he goes and runs off again. And now I find he's gone for good. Makes me look like some kind of sucker. Well, I'd like to tell him what I think of him, wasting my valuable time like that.

HAYAMI: But—

SASAKI: And the same goes for you, Mrs. Yamashita.

HAYAMI: But listen. (*He looks around the panel.*) Can we be sure that this time they *are* going to part? How does it strike you?

MORISAKI: Well, if he's really gone home, surely we can take that as final?

OGU: He's gone home, there's no question.

HAYAMI: (*Forcing a laugh:*) Makes you wonder what all the fuss was about. If he could turn around and go just like that, they shouldn't have caused all that trouble in the first place.

KAY: You're quite right. It's beyond me. If I loved a man enough to run off with him and abandon my children, I'd see it through to the very end.

MORISAKI: Otherwise why leave home?

FUJIWARA: Ah yes, that's what you ladies think, but love's like that, isn't it? It makes no sense to anyone else.

MORISAKI: That's true.

SASAKI: It's all very well doing crazy things because you're in love and can't help it, but where would society be if we all acted like that?

FUJIWARA: Of course. We all have our social responsibilities. Society makes us carry them out. That's how society works.

SASAKI: Well, someone who doesn't show up isn't worth worrying about. We can forget him. So, Mrs. Yamashita, what do you think of the situation? (*No answer.*) Mrs. Yamashita, I'm asking you.

FUKUKO: Yes.

SASAKI: Listen. Mr. Kakimoto has gone home. When you put it like that it doesn't sound so bad, but look at it this way: he's deserted you. Run off. Hasn't he?

FUKUKO: I don't think 'run off' is . . . (*She looks uncertain.*)

SASAKI: Well, I can understand you wouldn't want to think of it that way. But the fact is he has run off. And now what do you plan to do?

FUKUKO: (*She keeps her eyes lowered.*)

SASAKI: Are you going back to your husband?

FUKUKO: (*Glancing quickly at Yamashita:*) I want a separation.

OGU: Then you don't want to stay with Mr. Yamashita, either?

FUKUKO: No.

SASAKI: Mr. Yamashita, will you settle for that?

YAMASHITA: No, I want her back where she belongs.

FUKUKO: (*Lifting her head:*) Will you give me a divorce?

YAMASHITA: What about the kids? Don't tell me you've still got your head full of those ideas. Come on.

FUKUKO: I'll take them.

YAMASHITA: You're crazy. You think I'd let you take the kids? You couldn't even feed them. And the kids won't stand for it, for a start. Just you think about what you've done to them, you little—

SASAKI: Mr. Yamashita, Mr. Yamashita. Please. We won't get anywhere if you bring that up again, will we?

HAYAMI: You know, Mr. Yamashita, in view of everything that's happened I really think you two might be better off apart.

KAY: Quite right. And judging by the state Mrs. Yamashita's in, I'd say that's the best thing for the children, too. Why don't you each make a fresh start?

YAMASHITA: (*He looks offended.*)

FUJIWARA: Now how could he possibly accept that? Hmm?

YAMASHITA: No way. That'd be adding insult to injury.

SASAKI: That's true. You want to let bygones be bygones, don't you? And you've been telling your wife all along to come home.

HAYAMI: This Mr.—Kakimoto, is it? I hope he at least had the decency to pay Mrs. Yamashita's hospital bill?

YAMASHITA: Hell no! You think he's got the decency to do that?

OGU: That's—

HAYAMI: Good God, then you mean to tell me *you* paid? That's scandalous.

YAMASHITA: No, it was this—

OGU: The real problem is that they broke their promise and disappeared again. (*He presses hard on Yamashita's shoulder.*)

YAMASHITA: Right.

SASAKI: There's another problem, though. How did Mr. Kakimoto know where the hospital was? As I understand it, the only people who were supposed to know were the Yamashitas and Mrs. Yamashita's sister, who lives here in Tokyo. Now Mr. Yamashita is hardly likely to have told him. Did you, Mrs. Yamashita?

FUKUKO: No.

SASAKI: So that leaves only Mrs. Yamashita's sister, doesn't it?

OGU: Well—

SASAKI: That was a wicked thing to do. You see, I had the impression that Mr. Kakimoto had firmly made up his mind, and I expect he would have kept his word if he hadn't found out the hospital's address.

OGU: Yes, well—

YAMASHITA: Some kind of sister she turned out to be. So she helped break up our home, eh? The two of you ganged up against me!

OGU: (*While the camera is on Yamashita, he whispers to Sasaki to get off this topic.*) Just a minute, please. Let's leave what's already happened and talk about something a little more constructive.

SASAKI: Yes, yes, we must talk about the future.

OGU: We'll be back right after this message. In the meantime please try to calm yourself, Mr. Yamashita.

The usual commercial follows irrelevantly. Meanwhile Ogu forewarns the panelists to whom he will direct his next question. The others keep their eyes averted from Mr. and Mrs. Yamashita.

OGU: Now then, Mrs. Noto and Mr. Kawamura. Matters seem to be taking a legal turn here. What solutions might be available under the law?

NOTO: Well, before I can answer that I have a question: if the couple were to separate, in a case like this Mrs. Yamashita would naturally be expected to make some sort of recompense. Are you quite sure you want a separation, Mrs. Yamashita, even if you have to make a settlement?

FUKUKO: Yes.

NOTO: Then in view of the events that have led to the separation, Mr. Yamashita could reasonably expect a maximum of around three million yen.

HAYAMI: But surely she can't pay. She's not even working.

KAWAMURA: How about it, Mrs. Yamashita?

FUKUKO: I couldn't pay it immediately. But I'll do everything I can.

YAMASHITA: That's not good enough. If a separation is what you're after I've got to have the money in hard cash.

FUKUKO: I can't do the impossible.

YAMASHITA: *You're* impossible! You're in the wrong here and don't you forget it! Whose fault is it anyway?

FUKUKO: I've said I'll do everything I can.

SASAKI: (*After looking at Fukuko for a moment:*) Now you listen to me. Mr. Yamashita can't accept your word. Even I can't believe you're sincere if all you can offer is an IOU.

NOTO: That's very true. As you are at fault here, you'll have to provide some more definite proof of your sincerity.

YAMASHITA: Why not borrow the money from your sister? Or your parents?

KAWAMURA: Isn't there some way you could borrow the money?

FUKUKO: (*She shakes her head.*)

OGU: (*Turning to the panel:*) I should explain that since the incident Mrs. Yamashita has been estranged from her family. They won't agree to meet representatives from this program, either.

YAMASHITA: Hah! They're only pretending to cut her off so they won't have to part with any of their money.

NOTO: Under the circumstances would you be prepared to ask them for a loan?

FUKUKO: I can't.

KAWAMURA: Then nobody is going to believe you're sincere if all you can say is that you'll do what you can, but you're not even prepared to borrow the money.

SASAKI: Why don't you ask them? You never know, they might lend you the money.

FUKUKO: I don't want to cause my parents any more trouble.

SASAKI: Hah! (*The lawyers and Morisaki smile dryly.*)

YAMASHITA: Listen to you! What about all the trouble you've caused *me*, then? What about everything the kids and my mother have been through?

NOTO: He's right, my dear. Isn't it normal to think of that first?

HAYAMI: I wonder if it's right to put all the blame on her. The man who ran off with her is also responsible, isn't he?

KAWAMURA: Of course. Morally and legally.

KAY: That's as it should be.

HAYAMI: He can't be allowed to get off scot-free.

SASAKI: What about it, Mr. Yamashita?

YAMASHITA: If it comes to a divorce, I'll expect plenty of compensation from Kakimoto.

FUJIWARA: But surely he's in the same circumstances as Mrs. Yamashita? He won't be able to pay a sum that would satisfy Mr. Yamashita.

SASAKI: Then Mr. Yamashita must turn the other cheek? Is that what we're saying?

FUJIWARA: No, far from it. But let's be practical.

SASAKI: If we're being practical, it's not Mr. Yamashita's concern whether or not they can pay. Is it?

FUJIWARA: True.

SASAKI: They'll simply have to come up with the money between them. They have to pay for what they've done.

OGU: If your wife makes an immediate settlement of three million yen, Mr. Yamashita, will you agree to a divorce?

YAMASHITA: Well, it's not a thing you can settle with money. . . .

SASAKI: But there's no other way.

YAMASHITA: Well, yes, but . . .

SASAKI: Money's the only way you'll ever get this cleared up now, isn't it?

YAMASHITA: *If* it's paid on the line by her and Kakimoto, I'll agree to a divorce. I can tell you (*to Fukuko*), I've had to close up the shop because of you, and make all these trips to Tokyo, and spend money like nobody's business. (*To Sasaki:*) I've spent a cool million and a half. I'm in debt to loan sharks, to tell you the truth.

SASAKI: Then why not get your wife and Kakimoto to take on your repayments? How about it, Mrs. Yamashita? (*Fukuko licks her lips but does not reply.*) That's not getting us anywhere. You must have something to say. (*He leans back in his chair as if giving up.*)

HAYAMI: Mrs. Yamashita, isn't it the truth of the matter that you want to come back?

MORISAKI: You know, I do get the impression she's being a little stubborn to save her pride.

HAYAMI: If it weren't for your stubborn pride, Mr. Yamashita wouldn't be making such an issue of the settlement. If you'd simply apologize and come back, he'd let bygones be bygones. Isn't that right, Mr. Yamashita?

YAMASHITA: That's what I've said all along.

HAYAMI: And there'd be no further trouble. Everything will be just as it was before.

YAMASHITA: Well, I'm only human. It won't be exactly like it was before, but I'll keep quiet for the children's sake. She is their mother after all, whatever she's done, and it's better for them to have her there.

FUJIWARA: No wonder she's reluctant to come back with you talking like that.

SASAKI: Well so she should be. If she's holding out to save her pride, all I can say is grow up!

The camera cuts to the hosts and the sound from the round table fades out. Hidaka and Akari stand side by side before their desk.

HIDAKA: (*Seriously and frankly:*) The discussion is still in progress. But of course this isn't the kind of problem one can solve in a day. I've been married twenty years myself—I don't know how we've managed to do it. Because when you come down to it, the partners in a marriage are two separate individuals. Some strife will be inevitable along the way. What really counts, you know, is not to worry too much about appearances or what people will think, but to ask what's best for the marriage so that both partners and the children can live in the greatest health and happiness. Don't you think so, Akari?

AKARI: Yes, I do. Though it's easy for us to talk when we're on the outside—

HIDAKA: Of course it is. When one is personally involved, the emotion of the moment can cloud one's judgment and lead to an outcome that may not be what one really intended. Which is why we've set up a program like this in the hope of gaining the objectivity that an independent viewpoint can provide.

AKARI: Yes. We'll be back in a moment with another viewer who would like our help in tracing someone dear to him. But first these messages.

The third commercial break follows. Ogu leaves the round table and stands beside Akari in front of the desk. Hidaka strolls over to one of the monitors. A florid-faced man of thirty-seven or thirty-eight is brought over by the floor director from a corner of the studio to stand beside Ogu. He gazes around. The cue is given.

OGU: Well, today another of our viewers has an appeal to make. Welcome to the program, sir.

MAN: Thank you.

OGU: (*Looking at his notes:*) Mr. Koichi Izumi is thirty-seven years of age and works in the construction industry. The party he wants to locate is his wife, Yoshiko. (*A photograph of a woman's face, fuzzy from overenlargement, appears on-screen. Ogu's eyes go back and forth from the monitor to his notes.*) Yoshiko was missing suddenly on the third of this month. From various circumstances Mr. Izumi could only conclude that she had left home, and after trying every possible method to locate her, he contacted us. (*The camera returns.*)

AKARI: It must be a great worry to you.

OGU: Do you have any idea where she might be?

MAN: No, none.

OGU: Your wife is alone?

MAN: No. She used to work part-time, and a man from where she worked was missing on the same day.

OGU: Aha. Then they could very possibly be together?

MAN: Yes. They probably are.

OGU: (*He glances at Akari, who fails to speak.*) . . . Do you have children?

MAN: Yes, two.

OGU: That makes it especially hard on you. (*He glances again at Akari, gives up, and continues himself.*) . . . Does your wife have any identifying features? (*The woman's face reappears on the monitor.*)

MAN: She's five feet four inches and stocky. The nail on the little finger of her right hand was crushed in an accident. It's half missing.

OGU: That may be an important clue. (*The woman's photograph is replaced by a man's.*) And this is . . . ?

MAN: Yoshimoto, a college student, the guy I mentioned.

OGU: His name is Seiji Yoshimoto, I believe? And there's evidently a strong chance that he's with Mrs. Izumi. Could you describe him?

MAN: He's a little shrimp with an ugly way of talking.

OGU: Ah. (*The camera returns.*) Now, Mr. Izumi. Yoshiko could very well be watching this program. Would you like to face this camera and give her your message? Go ahead.

MAN: (*After a pause during which he looks into the lens:*) Come home, Yoshiko. The kids are missing school and we're miserable. You can do whatever you want. Let's *just* talk this over. This isn't solving anything. Come home, please, will you? (*He dries up and looks around confusedly at Ogu.*)

OGU: Well, now, if you're watching this program, Mrs. Yoshiko Izumi, please get in touch with us. And if anyone in our viewing audience has seen the missing persons, please give us a call at this number. (*The camera turns to the number that Akari is silently displaying.*) And now, a word from our sponsors.

The fourth commercial break follows. Hidaka returns to the desk and stands between Ogu and Akari. The floor director escorts the man away and wheels in a white telephone on a wagon. Ogu lifts the receiver and talks to the caller. The discussion at the round table continues intermittently. The commercials end.

OGU: Hello? . . . Yes . . . And you were in the store? (*A woman's excited voice is heard in the studio, disguised by a filter: "Yes, I live nearby and I'm sure it was them." The photographs are shown. "Yes, that's her. No mistaking it. Her little finger was like he said and everything."*) All right, now I'll pass you over to our secretary to give us the address. Thank you very much for your cooperation. (*He bows to the telephone and hangs up.*) Well, already information on Mrs. Izumi's whereabouts is beginning to come in.

HIDAKA: I see the discussion is still in progress. (*The camera briefly shows what's happening at the round table.*)

OGU: The problems don't seem to have been cleared up yet, do they? If you ask me, the only thing for Mrs. Yamashita to do now is give in with good grace. (*The camera returns.*)

HIDAKA: Well, the important thing is what she herself wants. It wouldn't do for us to make decisions for her, would it?

OGU: That's true. (*The theme song begins to play softly.*) The discussion between the Yamashitas is still going on, but we've run out of time. Next week we'll be talking about the Izumis' story. I hope Mrs. Izumi turns up—what do you think, Mr. Hidaka?

HIDAKA: The information seems to be coming in. I think she'll turn up.

AKARI: And tomorrow, on Wednesday, we have *People In Depth* featuring Dr. Daikichi Kazuka, the director of the Philanthropists Hospital, who is causing a furor in the Medical Association with his controversial methods of treatment.

HIDAKA: Until tomorrow, then. Have a good day.

The music grows louder. Some of the people on-screen remain at the table, others are already on their feet as the credits roll. An announcer's deadpan voice says, "This program has been brought to you by the following sponsors." Detergent and food trademarks follow rapidly, their size and the number of seconds they remain on-screen being determined by the amount each sponsor paid. Then a commercial flashes brightly on, not allowing the tiniest interruption.

THE LOBBY

Nobuo Koda descended from on high, down the steep metal stairs that linked the control room with the studio floor. Daisuke Kiyokawa and two or three members of the crew followed. Before Koda had reached the ground, Kazushi Hidaka, who'd been the first off the set, was out the door behind the staircase. Kiyokawa and the crew moved toward the set while Koda stood watching in the doorway.

The set was softly illuminated through the layer of dust. People were leaving the pool of soft light and walking, some briskly, some at leisure, toward the door.

As they passed Koda they made an assortment of polite remarks, then stepped one by one into the brightly lit corridor. Some paused for a brief conversation. Koda replied to each. Kojiro Sasaki came up with his hands thrust into his trouser pockets.

"Great show," he said, raising a hand in greeting. Then he stopped, motioned with his chin, and pulled a face. "Hopeless couple." He went out laughing sardonically.

Takao Yamashita approached swaying from side to side at each step; Fukuko was a few paces behind with Kiyokawa. They stopped in front of Koda.

"Thanks for coming in." Unusual for him, Koda was all smiles.

"I'm much obliged to you." Yamashita bowed his head deeply, and as Fukuko caught up, with Kiyokawa in between, she lowered her head, too, as if in unconscious imitation. Akari came to a stop a little off to one side. Koda's eyes went back and forth between Mr. and Mrs. Yamashita. "Now," he said, "it's up to the two of you to talk it over yourselves and find the best solution."

"Yes, we know. So next time you're having that Mr. Izumi on?" said Yamashita compliantly. Koda's expression returned to normal.

"Yes. We receive far more requests than we can cope with. If we were to be involved with one case for too long it would be unfair. But the panelists have put a good deal of time and effort into advising you, haven't they, Mr. Yamashita?"

"Oh yes. Thank you very much." After another deep bow, Yamashita raised dazed-looking eyes to Koda. "We're going to settle it between us two."

"I'm glad." With a pointed glance at his wristwatch Koda added, "I'm afraid I can't keep you company as I have work to do."

"Oh yes, we know. Do you think you could possibly arrange somewhere for us to go?"

"Ah." Koda looked up at the ceiling and answered, "Well, if it's not for more than two or three hours we can let you have the use of the Mitaya. Your wife knows where it is. Kiyokawa, telephone the owner, will you?"

"Thank you."

"Now I must be going. Please collect the fees for your appearance from Mr. Kiyokawa. We've included transportation to Osaka for your wife as well, should she require it."

"That's very good of you."

"Kiyokawa, will you see the Yamashitas out? Be back at your desk as soon as possible. I want to leave with the film crew at two."

Led by Kiyokawa, the Yamashitas left the studio. Koda was close behind them when Akari caught up to him.

"Excuse me, Mr. Koda—"

"Ah, Miss Kasai. What happened to you today? Mr. Ogu had to cover for you. You weren't following the script, were you?"

"That's what I wanted to speak to you about."

Just as they reached the corridor Koda's attention was distracted by the appearance of Kenichi Tendo at its other end. Tendo was walking fast in their direction and hailed them with a smile from some distance away: "Everything went off beautifully, I see. I was watching in my office. The phone calls are jamming the switchboard again. You'd better get back to your desk."

He continued on down the corridor without slowing. Koda quickened his own pace. "Do you have a moment?"

"Not now. I'll be back about five."

"I'll be out with the crew then."

"What is it?"

"It's about the next case. There's something I'd like to discuss with you beforehand."

"No need, Mr. Koda. I'll leave everything to your excellent judgment." And he clapped Koda lightly on the back. Akari, trotting to keep up with them, forced herself to speak up.

"Please take me off the Tuesday program."

The men stopped in the middle of the lobby. They looked back at Akari. After glancing casually around, Tendo said, "You want to leave the Tuesday program?"

He stared piercingly at Akari. Returning his gaze, Akari nodded and said "Yes." A smile spread slowly over Tendo's face.

"You can't quit just the Tuesday program, you know."

"In that case I'm afraid I'll have to quit completely," Akari said as if reciting from memory.

"All right," came Tendo's prompt response.

"Wait." Koda's voice was trembling. "What's going on? Might I ask why you want to quit my program and only mine?"

"Forget it," Tendo said warningly. "Akari has told us she's quitting completely. Let's leave it at that."

"But she's signed on until September of next year. This is a breach of contract."

"Let's not be rigid. Now, if she were to leave us tomorrow we'd be in trouble and the studio would no doubt be forced to hold her to her contract. But that's not what you're suggesting, is it, Akari?"

With a suddenly apprehensive look, Akari gave a faint nod. Tendo went on unruffled to explain: "There's a clause in the contract requiring three months' notice by either party should they wish to cancel. And I believe there was also something about that notice being subject to the other party's acceptance where cancellation would be severely detrimental to said party's interests."

Akari was looking more and more intimidated. "Then I can't quit?"

"Of course you can quit," Tendo replied with a laugh. "But not tomorrow, and not if it's going to be severely detrimental to the station's interests."

Koda excused himself and stalked off toward the studio. Paying no attention to him, Tendo looked down amicably at Akari. "We'll be sorry to lose you, Akari. Hidaka will, especially."

Then he suddenly stooped to whisper melodiously in Akari's ear, "But it won't change a thing—no one can get out," and turned quickly away.

Akari involuntarily put her hand to her ear where the whispered words reverberated. Her eyes followed Tendo's departing back, and her mouth remained slightly open. When Tendo came to the middle of the wall of plate glass, the automatic doors parted respectfully as if they'd been waiting for him. He went out between them.

At the same time Akari recognized Kiyokawa standing off to the side of the automatic doors, unaware of Tendo. Kiyokawa had his face up against the glass. Outside, the entrance area was dark in the building's shadow. Beyond it lay a broad acacia-lined street. Kiyokawa was looking at a point outside, directly across the lobby from where Akari stood.

What he saw there, from behind, were the figures of Mr. and Mrs. Yamashita. Yamashita was grasping Fukuko's right elbow with his left hand. They moved forward like that. They weren't in step, which made Fukuko swing her hips, and her right shoulder stuck up oddly with the pressure of her husband's grasp. As the couple emerged from the studio's shadow, Tendo walked briskly across the area between them and the glass wall and disappeared toward the parking lot.

The couple crossed the sidewalk. Through the faintly tinted glass they seemed to be crossing the sandy floor of a shallow sun-filled sea. Perhaps it was the rippling of the water that made Yamashita's and Fukuko's backsides sway so comically. At the edge of the sidewalk Fukuko bent at the waist and her weight stopped Yamashita from crossing the road. Half turning, he put his foot back on the curb. With a jerk of her right arm, Fukuko twisted her elbow out of Yamashita's hand and straightened the rumpled shoulder and collar of her dress.

A car went by. Yamashita started to cross when it had gone. Fukuko stood still and watched him. A very heavy-looking canvas travel bag hung from her slack left arm. Her coat's lining sagged at the sleeve openings. A car passed between Fukuko and Yamashita. First one, and then another. They were moving at sufficient speed to smash a crumpled human can. Now Fukuko stepped out. Then she ran. A car obscured her for a second, and then she came into sight again as she made it to the opposite sidewalk, scrambling and waving her free hand.

Fukuko had arrived unscathed on the distant shore. She followed her husband silently, her jaw and her hip jutting out awkwardly until she drew level with him and they vanished down the side street that led to the Mitaya. All was well, too, on the inside of the glass wall. The receptionist's phone rang; a cart rattled past delivering coffee; people breezed by, ran into acquaintances with cries of delight, chatted on a sofa in the corner, and went on their way; and all the while pictures filled the screen of the imposing television set beside the sofa without the tiniest interruption.

Kiyokawa looked back slowly. There was a hint of puzzlement in the way he held his head. He was wearing a discontented frown and his lids were half lowered over his large eyes. Akari waited for Kiyokawa's gaze to reach her. Their eyes met. And then for some reason Kiyokawa blushed to the tips of his ears and rushed off to the studio.